DEBBIE MUMM®

I ♥ CARE
with Quilts

Sewing to Make
a Difference

• • •

©2009 by Debbie Mumm • Leisure Arts, Inc., 5701 Ranch Drive, Little Rock, AR 72223 • www.leisurearts.com

"The most giving and caring people on the planet are quilt makers. Quilters are always looking for opportunities through their craft to support people who are in need or are in need of comfort."

Planet Green Lap Quilt

Dear Friends,

The most giving and caring people on the planet are quilt makers. Quilters are always looking for opportunities through their craft to support people who are in need or are in need of comfort. This book focuses on quilts and projects that communicate a message of caring through design, color choices, or concepts. Whether it's to support a cause or charity that's near and dear to your heart, an ailing loved one, or a friend who needs a little extra TLC, the projects in this book tell a story of love and caring. Even better, all the projects are quick, uncomplicated, and a delight to sew so you'll be able to offer your generous aid to many.

While researching this book, we were struck by the many non-profit organizations that have been established to provide quilts for those in need. From Quilts for Kids and the Alzheimer's Art Quilt Initiative to American Hero Quilts for wounded servicemen, quilters are using their skills to bring comfort to others. We've mentioned a few of these foundations and organizations throughout this book, but many more exist to help you provide to those in need.

On a personal note, I'd like you to know that many of the quilts developed for this book will be donated to a variety of causes that are near and dear to our staff including diabetes, breast cancer research, Alzheimer's and Project Linus.

It is an honor for me to be associated with this wonderful, generous, kind, and creative group that we call "quilters."

Love,
Debbie Mumm

TABLE of Contents

Rescue

Remembrance

Good Fortune

Gratitude

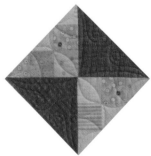

TLC

Heart to Heart

RESCUE
••• Lap Quilt

Rescue Lap Quilt Finished Size: 47¼" x 60"	FIRST CUT		SECOND CUT	
	Number of Strips or Pieces	Dimensions	Number of Pieces	Dimensions
Fabric A Background 1⅙ yards	2 3 1	14" x 42" 3½" x 42" 1½" x 42"	3 2 24 12	14" squares* *cut twice diagonally 7¼" squares** **cut once diagonally 3½" squares 3½" x 1½"
Fabric B Background 1⅛ yards	5 12	3½" x 42" 1½" x 42"	48	3½" squares
Fabric C Block 1 Accent Stripe ½ yard	10	1½" x 42"		
Fabric D Block 2 Accent Stripe ⅓ yard	6	1½" x 42"		
Fabric E Block 2 Center ⅙ yard	2	1½" x 42"	6	1½" x 3½"
First Border ⅓ yard	5	1½" x 42"		
Outside Border ⅔ yard	6	3½" x 42"		
Binding ⅝ yard	6	2¾" x 42"		
Backing - 3 yards Batting - 53" x 66"				

Fabric Requirements and Cutting Instructions

Read all instructions before beginning and use ¼"-wide seam allowances throughout. Read Cutting Strips and Pieces on page 92 prior to cutting fabric.

Getting Started

When unexpected emergencies happen this quilt will bring warmth and solace. Block measures 9½" square (unfinished). Refer to Accurate Seam Allowance on page 92. Whenever possible use Assembly Line Method on page 92. Press seams in direction of arrows.

Making Block 1

1. Sew lengthwise one 1½" x 42" Fabric B strip between two 1½" x 42" Fabric C strips as shown to make a strip set. Press seams toward Fabric C. Make five. Cut strip set into forty-eight 3½"-wide segments as shown.

3½

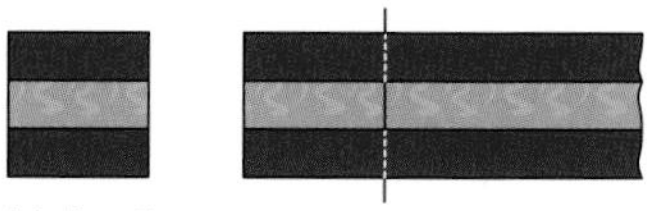

Make 5
Cut 48 segments

2. Sew lengthwise one 1½" x 42" Fabric A strip between two 1½" x 42" Fabric B strips as shown to make a strip set. Press seams toward Fabric A. Cut strip set into twenty-four 1½"-wide segments as shown.

1½

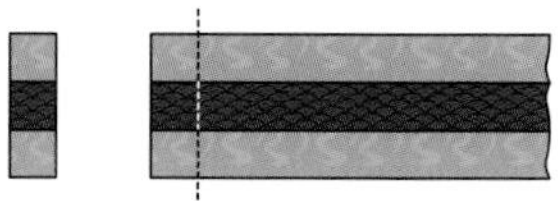

Cut 24 segments

Quilters have been donating quilts to the American Red Cross and other emergency service agencies for centuries and this large, flannel-backed, quilt is just-right to provide warmth and solace to those affected by natural and man-made disasters. Cross shapes are repeated in this easy-to-piece design.

3. Sew one 3½" x 1½" Fabric A piece between two units from step 2 as shown. Press. Make twelve.

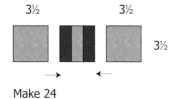

Make 12

4. Sew one unit from step 1 between two 3½" Fabric B squares as shown. Press. Make twenty-four.

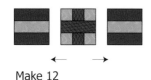

Make 24

5. Sew one unit from step 3 between two units from step 1 as shown. Press. Make twelve.

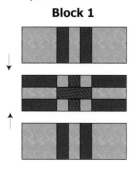

Make 12

6. Sew one unit from step 5 between two units from step 4 as shown. Press. Make twelve and label Block 1. Block measures 9½" square.

Block 1

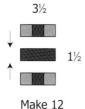

Make 12
Block measures 9½"

Making Block 2

1. Sew lengthwise one 1½" x 42" Fabric B strip between two 1½" x 42" Fabric D strips as shown to make a strip set. Press seams toward Fabric B. Make three. Cut strip set into twenty-four 3½"-wide segments as shown.

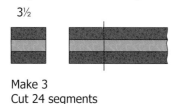

Make 3
Cut 24 segments

2. Sew lengthwise one 1½" x 42" Fabric E strip between two 1½" x 42" Fabric B strips as shown to make a strip set. Press seams toward Fabric B. Cut strip set into twelve 1½"-wide segments as shown.

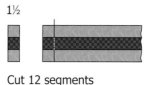

Cut 12 segments

3. Sew one 1½" x 3½" Fabric E piece between two units from step 2 as shown. Press. Make six.

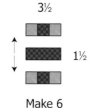

Make 6

4. Sew one unit from step 1 between two 3½" Fabric A squares as shown. Press. Make twelve.

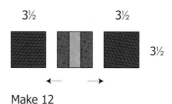

Make 12

5. Sew one unit from step 3 between two units from step 1 as shown. Press. Make six.

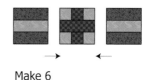

Make 6

6. Sew one unit from step 5 between two units from step 4 as shown. Press. Make six and label Block 2. Block measures 9½" square.

Block 2

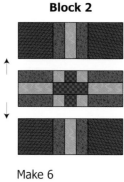

Make 6
Block measures 9½"

Assembly

1. Sew one small Fabric A triangle to one Block 1. Triangle ends will extend past block edges. Press. Sew this unit between two large Fabric A triangles as shown. Press. Make two and label Rows 1 and 6.

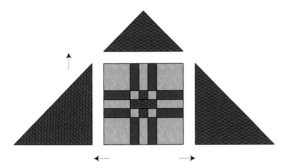

Make 2, label Rows 1 & 6

2. Arrange and sew together two large Fabric A triangles, two of Block 1, and one of Block 2 as shown. Press. Make two and label Rows 2 and 5.

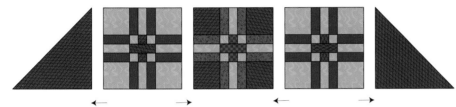

Make 2, label Rows 2 & 5

3. Arrange and sew together one small Fabric A triangle, three of Block 1, two of Block 2, and one large Fabric A triangle as shown. Press. Make two and label Rows 3 and 4.

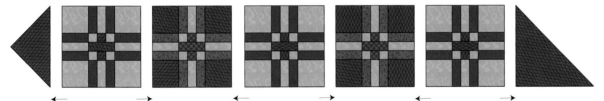

Make 2, label Rows 3 & 4

4. Referring to photo on page 7 and layout on page 10, arrange and sew rows 1-6 together. Press.

Adding the Borders

1. Refer to Adding the Borders on page 94. Sew 1½" x 42" First Border strips together end-to-end to make one continuous 1½"-wide First Border strip. Measure quilt through center from side to side. Cut two 1½"-wide First Border strips to this measurement. Sew to top and bottom of quilt. Press seams toward border.

2. Measure quilt through center from top to bottom including border just added. Cut two 1½"-wide First Border strips to this measurement. Sew to sides of quilt. Press.

3. Refer to steps 1 and 2 to join, measure, trim, and sew 3½"-wide Outside Border strips to top, bottom, and sides of quilt. Press.

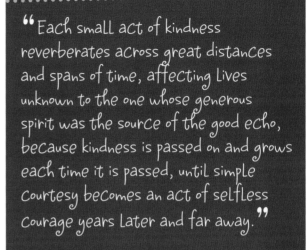

"Each small act of kindness reverberates across great distances and spans of time, affecting lives unknown to the one whose generous spirit was the source of the good echo, because kindness is passed on and grows each time it is passed, until simple courtesy becomes an act of selfless courage years later and far away."

Dean Koontz
The Character of H.R. White in "From the Corner of His Eye"

Quilters Care

....to Provide Comfort and Warmth in Emergencies

In the midst of a trauma, quilts provide comfort, warmth, and hope to those in distress. Whether it's a fire, flood, natural disaster, accident, or other crisis, a quilt is something to hang on to in an emergency.

Over the years quilters have made many quilts for the American Red Cross to warm disaster victims, refugees and others in need. Check with your local chapter on the need in your area.

State and local police often welcome donated quilts. Police in some communities carry them in the trunk for use if children need to be removed from a home in domestic situations or at an accident to provide comfort on the scene. Check with your local police departments to see if there is a program in your area. Be sure to check on any size requirements.

During times of disaster, Fire Stations act as a conduit to get supplies to those in need and in some areas quilt guilds team up with fire department to provide quilts to help victims through traumatic situations. Call your local fire station to see if quilts are needed in your area.

Homeless shelters and missions need utilitarian quilts for beds especially in the wintertime. Fundraising is an on-going challenge for many shelters. Contact your local shelter or mission to see if there is an opportunity to donate an intricate quilt for a raffle or auction to help raise funds.

Layering and Finishing

1. Cut backing crosswise into two equal pieces. Sew pieces together lengthwise to make one 54" x 80" (approximate) backing piece. Press and trim to 54" x 66".

2. Referring to Layering the Quilt on page 94, arrange and baste backing, batting, and top together. Hand or machine quilt as desired.

3. Refer to Binding the Quilt on page 94. Sew 2¾" x 42" binding strips end-to-end to make one continuous 2¾"-wide binding strip. Bind quilt to finish.

Rescue Lap Quilt
Finished Size: 47¼" x 60"

RESCUE
··· Quilt Bag

Present your quilt in this easy-to-make quilt bag. Create a special label if desired, and attach to top of bag. The bag can be used as a pillowcase when the quilt is in use.

Rescue Quilt Bag Finished Size: 18" x 29½"	FIRST CUT	
	Number of Strips or Pieces	Dimensions
Bag 1 yard	1	30½" x 36½"
Bag Accent ¼ yard	1	5" x 36½"
Cording - 1½ yards		

Making the Quilt Bag

Read all directions before beginning and use ¼"-wide seam allowances throughout.

1. Sew 5" x 36½" Fabric B piece to 30½" x 36½" Fabric A piece. Press.

2. On the 36½" Fabric A side, fold under ¼" to the wrong side. Press. Measure from folded edge and fold under 4¾" to the wrong side. Press. Unfold for next step.

3. With right sides together, sew along long edge and bottom of bag (edge with accent strip). Clip corners, turn right side out, and press.

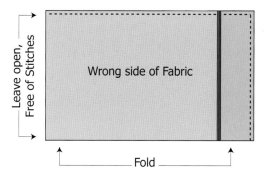

Leave open, Free of Stitches

Wrong side of Fabric

Fold

4. Repress top fold to inside of bag along both the ¼" and 4¾" pressed edges. Top stitch close to pressed edges.

5. Insert quilt into bag and tie with cording close to top-stitched line as shown in photo.

Good Fortune
··· Wall Quilt

Good Fortune Wall Quilt Finished Size: 45" x 45"	FIRST CUT		SECOND CUT	
	Number of Strips or Pieces	Dimensions	Number of Pieces	Dimensions
Fabric A Tulip Background & Garden Path Block ⅝ yard	2 2	6½" x 42" 2" x 42"	5 8 4	6½" x 12½" 2" x 4¼" 2" squares
Fabric B Ladybug Background & Garden Path Block ⅜ yard	1 2	6½" x 42" 2" x 42"	5 8 4	6½" squares 2" x 4¼" 2" squares
Fabric C Ladybug Background & Garden Path Block ⅜ yard	1 2	6½" x 42" 2" x 42"	5 8 4	6½" squares 2" x 4¼" 2" squares
Fabric D Garden Path Corners ⅓ yard	2	4¼" x 42"	16	4¼" squares
Fabric E Garden Path Block ⅙ yard	2	2" x 42"	8 8	2" x 4¼" 2" squares
Fabric F Garden Path Block ⅙ yard	2	2" x 42"	8 4	2" x 4¼" 2" squares
Fabric G Garden Path Block ⅛ yard	1	2" x 42"	4 4	2" x 4¼" 2" squares
Fabric H Garden Path Block ⅛ yard	1	2" x 42"	4 8	2" x 4¼" 2" squares
First Border ¼ yard	4	1½" x 42"		
Outside Border ⅝ yard	5	3½" x 42"		
Binding ½ yard	5	2¾" x 42"		
Tulip & Ladybug Appliqués - Six assorted fat quarters Backing - 2⅞ yards Batting - 51" x 51" Lightweight Fusible Web - 1½ yards				

Fabric Requirements and Cutting Instructions

Read all instructions before beginning and use ¼"-wide seam allowances throughout. Read Cutting Strips and Pieces on page 92 prior to cutting fabric.

Getting Started

This cheerful quilt is sure to bring lots of smiles. Blocks measure 12½" square (unfinished). Refer to Accurate Seam Allowance on page 92. Whenever possible use Assembly Line Method on page 92. Press seams in direction of arrows.

Making the Garden Blocks

Refer to appliqué instructions on page 93. Our instructions are for Quick-Fuse Appliqué, but if you prefer hand appliqué, reverse templates and add ¼"-wide seam allowances.

1. Sew one 6½" Fabric B square to one 6½" Fabric C square. Press. Sew this unit to one 6½" x 12½" Fabric A piece as shown. Press. Make five.

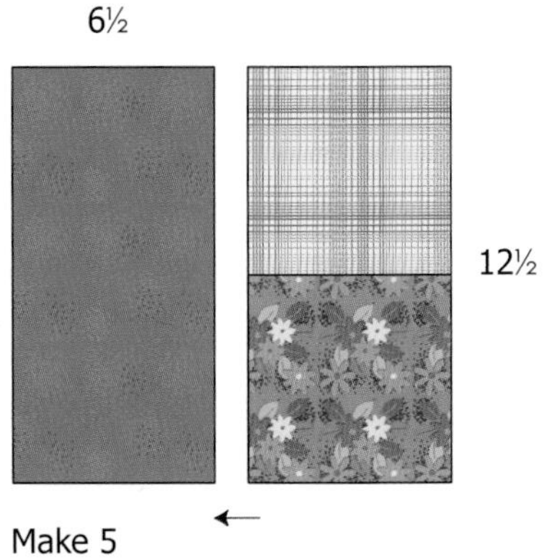

6½

12½

Make 5

2. Use pattern on page 15 to trace tulip, leaves, and ladybug's body and wings on paper side of fusible web. Use appropriate fabrics to prepare all appliqués for fusing.

3. Refer to photo to position and fuse appliqués to unit from step 1. Finish appliqué edges with machine satin stitch or other decorative stitching as desired. Garden Block measures 12½" square.

Brighten anyone's day with this light-hearted quilt featuring springtime tulips and our favorite ladybugs. Pick a pretty floral as your inspiration and develop your color palette around it. Ladybugs are thought to bring luck in nearly all cultures and French lore states that if a ladybug lands on you, you'll have good fortune. Be sure to pass this folklore on to the lucky person who gets this quilt!

Making the Garden Path Blocks

1. Sew one 2" x 4¼" Fabric G piece between one 2" x 4¼" Fabric A and one 2" x 4¼" Fabric E piece as shown. Press. Make four and label Unit 1. Repeat step to make four each of the following combinations; 2" x 4¼" Fabric E, F, and H for Unit 2, 2" x 4¼" Fabric C, B, and A for Unit 3, and 2" x 4¼" Fabric F, B, and C for Unit 4.

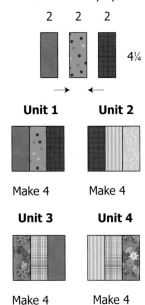

Unit 1 **Unit 2**

Make 4   Make 4

Unit 3 **Unit 4**

Make 4   Make 4

2. Refer to diagram below to arrange 2" Fabric A, B, C, E, F, G, and H squares in three rows with three squares each. Sew squares together into rows. Press. Sew rows together and press. Make four.

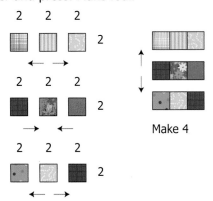

Make 4

3. Sew one Unit 1 between two 4¼" Fabric D squares as shown. Press. Make four. Sew one Unit 4 between two 4¼" Fabric D squares. Press. Make four.

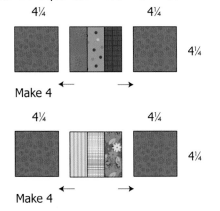

Make 4

Make 4

4. Sew one unit from step 2 between one Unit 2 and one Unit 3 as shown. Press. Make four.

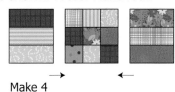

Make 4

5. Sew one unit from step 4 between two units from step 3, one of each combination as shown. Press. Make four. Block measures 12½" square.

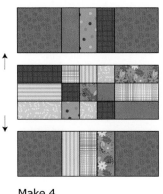

Make 4
Block measures 12½ square

Assembling the Quilt

1. Referring to photo on page 13, sew one Garden Path Block between two Garden Blocks. Press toward Garden Block. Make two.

2. Sew one Garden Block between two Garden Path Blocks. Press toward Garden Block. Sew rows together. Press.

Adding the Borders

1. Refer to Adding the Borders on page 94. Measure quilt through center from side to side. Cut two 1½"-wide First Border strips to this measurement. Sew to top and bottom of quilt. Press seams toward border.

2. Measure quilt through center from top to bottom including border just added. Cut two 1½"-wide First Border strips to this measurement. Sew to sides of quilt. Press.

3. Refer to steps 1 and 2 to measure, trim, and sew 3½"-wide Outside Border strips to top and bottom of quilt. Press. Sew remaining 3½" x 42" Outside Border strips to make one continuous 3½"-wide strip. Press. Measure quilt through center from side to side. Cut two Outside Border strips to this measurement and sew to sides of quilt. Press.

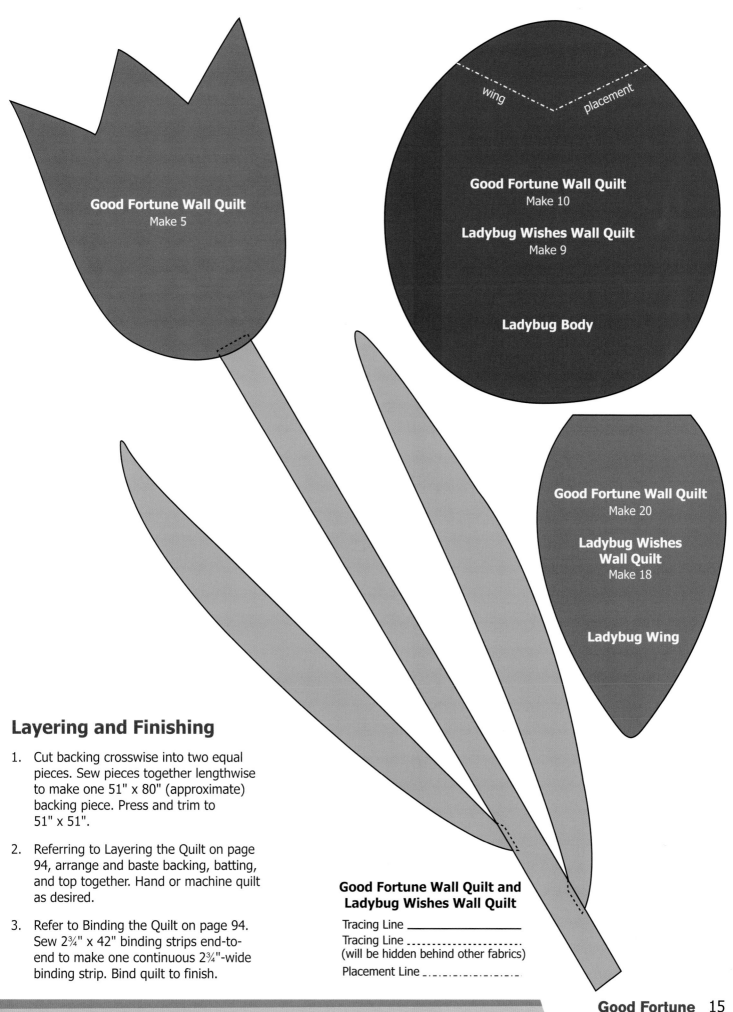

Good Fortune Wall Quilt
Make 5

Good Fortune Wall Quilt
Make 10

Ladybug Wishes Wall Quilt
Make 9

Ladybug Body

wing   placement

Good Fortune Wall Quilt
Make 20

**Ladybug Wishes
Wall Quilt**
Make 18

Ladybug Wing

Layering and Finishing

1. Cut backing crosswise into two equal pieces. Sew pieces together lengthwise to make one 51" x 80" (approximate) backing piece. Press and trim to 51" x 51".

2. Referring to Layering the Quilt on page 94, arrange and baste backing, batting, and top together. Hand or machine quilt as desired.

3. Refer to Binding the Quilt on page 94. Sew 2¾" x 42" binding strips end-to-end to make one continuous 2¾"-wide binding strip. Bind quilt to finish.

**Good Fortune Wall Quilt and
Ladybug Wishes Wall Quilt**

Tracing Line _____
Tracing Line _ _ _ _ _ _ _ _ _ _ _ _ _
(will be hidden behind other fabrics)
Placement Line _ . _ . _ . _ . _ . _ . _

Ladybug Wishes ... Wall Quilt

Ladybug Wishes Wall Quilt Finished Size: 19" x 20"	FIRST CUT		SECOND CUT	
	Number of Strips or Pieces	Dimensions	Number of Pieces	Dimensions
Fabric A Background ¼ yard	1	6½" x 42"	5	6½" squares
Fabric B Background ¼ yard	1	6½" x 42"	4	6½" squares
Fabric C Accent ⅛ yard	1	1" x 42"	2	1" x 18½"
Binding ¼ yard each of 2 fabrics	2*	2¾" x 42" *cut for each fabric		

Ladybug Appliqués - Assorted Scraps**
Backing - ⅔ yard
Batting - 24" x 24"
Lightweight Fusible Web - ⅝ yard
*Note: we used Fabric A & C for project binding strips.
**We used 7 different fabrics for ladybugs.

Fabric Requirements and Cutting Instructions

Read all instructions before beginning and use ¼"-wide seam allowances throughout. Read Cutting Strips and Pieces on page 92 prior to cutting fabric.

Getting Started

Refer to Accurate Seam Allowance on page 92. Whenever possible use Assembly Line Method on page 92. Press seams in direction of arrows.

Making the Quilt

1. Sew one 6½" Fabric B square between two 6½" Fabric A squares as shown. Press. Make two.

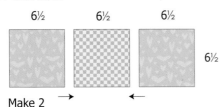

Make 2

2. Sew one 6½" Fabric A square between two 6½" Fabric B squares as shown. Press.

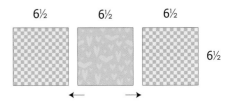

3. Referring to photo, sew together two 1" x 18½" Fabric C strips and rows from steps 1 and 2. Press seams toward Fabric C.

Adding the Appliqués

Refer to appliqué instructions on page 93. Our instructions are for Quick-Fuse Appliqué, but if you prefer hand appliqué, reverse templates and add ¼"-wide seam allowances.

1. Use patterns on page 15 to trace ladybug wings and bodies on paper side of fusible web. Use appropriate fabrics to prepare all appliqués for fusing.

2. Refer to photo to position and fuse appliqués to quilt. Finish appliqué edges with machine satin stitch or other decorative stitching as desired.

Layering and Finishing

1. Referring to Layering the Quilt on page 94, arrange and baste backing, batting, and top together. Hand or machine quilt as desired.

2. Two different fabrics were used to bind this quilt. Refer to photo for binding placement. Refer to Binding the Quilt on page 94. Use 2¾"-wide Binding strips to bind quilt.

If ladybugs are lucky, the person who gets this quilt will be truly blessed! Nine jaunty ladybugs land on a sweet little quilt bringing wishes for health, happiness, and good fortune. A contemporary color palette adds a hint of sophistication to these lucky bugs.

TLC ···Lap Quilt

TLC Lap Quilt Finished Size: 47" x 59"	FIRST CUT		SECOND CUT	
	Number of Strips or Pieces	Dimensions	Number of Pieces	Dimensions
Fabric A Block 1 Nine-Patch ½ yard each of 3 light fabrics	1* 2*	7" x 42" 2½" x 42" *cut for each fabric	3*	7" squares
Fabric B Block 1 Nine-Patch ⅓ yard each of 3 light fabrics	1* 1*	7" x 42" 2½" x 42" *cut for each fabric	3*	7" squares
Fabric C Block 2 Nine-Patch ½ yard each of 3 dark fabrics	1* 2*	7" x 42" 2½" x 42" *cut for each fabric	3*	7" squares
Fabric D Block 2 Nine-Patch ⅓ yard each of 3 dark fabrics	1* 1*	7" x 42" 2½" x 42" *cut for each fabric	3*	7" squares
First Border ⅛ yard each of 6 dark fabrics	1*	1½" x 42" *cut for each fabric	3*	1½" x 13½"
Outside Border ⅓ yard	6	1½" x 42"		
Binding ⅝ yard	6	2¾" x 42"		
Backing - 3 yards Batting - 53" x 65"				

Fabric Requirements and Cutting Instructions

Read all instructions before beginning and use ¼"-wide seam allowances throughout. Read Cutting Strips and Pieces on page 92 prior to cutting fabric.

Getting Started

Need a quilt in a hurry? Go to your fabric stash and make this easy to construct quilt in record time! Blocks measure 6½" square (unfinished). Refer to Accurate Seam Allowance on page 92. Whenever possible use Assembly Line Method on page 92. Press seams in direction of arrows.

Making the Half-Square Triangles

Draw a diagonal line on wrong side of one 7" Fabric A or Fabric B square. Place marked square and one 7" Fabric C or D square right sides together. Sew scant ¼" away from drawn line on both sides to make half-square triangles as shown. Make eighteen using an assortment of fabric squares. Cut on drawn line and press. Square to 6½" and label Block 1. This will make thirty-six of Block 1. You will need thirty-two for this project.

Fabric A or B = 7 x 7
Fabric C or D = 7 x 7
Make 18

Block 1

→
Square to 6½
Make 36
Half-square Triangles
(32 will be used for this project.)

Making the Nine-Patch Blocks

1. Sew together lengthwise one 2½" x 42" Fabric B strip and two 2½" x 42" Fabric A strips as shown to make a strip set. Press seams in one direction. Make three in assorted arrangements. Cut strip sets into forty-five 2½"-wide segments as shown.

2½

Make 3
Cut 45 segments

Show you care with an eye-catching quilt that gives the illusion of diagonal construction. A captivating color combination and strategic placement of lights and darks makes this handsome quilt look far more complicated than it is——making it the perfect quilt to whip up for a friend or family member that needs a little TLC.

2. Arrange three assorted units from step 1 as shown. Repress seams as needed. Sew units together and press. Make fifteen and label Block 2. Block measures 6½" square.

Block 2

Make 15
Block measures 6 ½" square

3. Sew together lengthwise one 2½" x 42" Fabric D strip and two 2½" x 42" Fabric C strips as shown to make a strip set. Press seams in one direction. Make three in assorted arrangements. Cut strip sets into forty-eight 2½"-wide segments as shown.

2½

Make 3
Cut 48 segments

4. Arrange three assorted units from step 3 as shown. Repress seams as needed. Sew units together and press. Make sixteen and label Block 3. Block measures 6½" square.

Block 3

Make 16
Block measures 6 ½" square

Assembling the Quilt

Since this quilt has a scrappy look you will need to refer to photo on page 19 and layout on page 21 to arrange all blocks into nine rows with seven blocks each before proceeding to step instructions. This allows the play of different blocks in a variety of positions to obtain the desired overall effect.

1. Arrange and sew together four of Block 1, two of Block 3 and one of Block 2. Press. Make three and label Rows 1, 5, and 9.

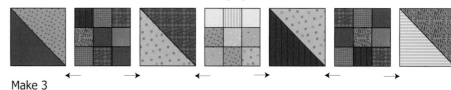

Make 3
Label Rows 1, 5 & 9

2. Arrange and sew together two of Block 2, three of Block 1 and two of Block 3 as shown. Press. Make four, and label Rows 2 and 6 as shown. Rotate remaining rows so Block 3 is to the left and label Rows 4 and 8.

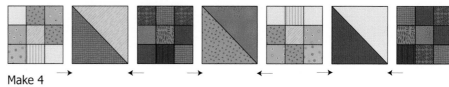

Make 4
Label two Rows 2 & 6
Rotate two rows and label Rows 4 & 8

3. Arrange and sew together four of Block 1, two of Block 2 and one of Block 3. Press. Make two.

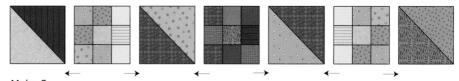

Make 2
Label Rows 3 & 7

4. Referring to photo on page 19 and layout on page 21, arrange and sew rows together. Press.

Adding the Borders

1. Sew 1½" x 13½" assorted First Border strips together end-to-end to make one continuous border strip. Press.

2. Refer to Adding the Borders on page 94. Measure quilt through center from side to side. Cut two 1½"-wide First Border strips to this measurement. Sew to top and bottom of quilt. Press seams toward border.

3. Measure quilt through center from top to bottom including border just added. Cut two 1½"-wide First Border strips to this measurement. Sew to sides of quilt. Press.

4. Refer to steps 1 and 2 to join, measure, trim, and sew 1½"-wide Outside Border strips to top, bottom, and sides of quilt. Press.

Layering and Finishing

1. Cut backing crosswise into two equal pieces. Sew pieces together lengthwise to make one 53" x 80" (approximate) backing piece. Press and trim to 53" x 65".

2. Referring to Layering the Quilt on page 94, arrange and baste backing, batting, and top together. Hand or machine quilt as desired.

TLC Lap Quilt
Finished Size: 47" x 59"

Quilters Care
• • • **with a handmade card**

Scraps of pretty papers, ribbons, beads, buttons, and scrapbook letters are all you need to create handmade cards to accompany your gift quilts. Use appliqué patterns as templates for cutting your paper for the tulip and ladybug cards. Create bands of color and texture with ribbons for the "hi" card. Add rub-on or embossed letters and embellish with ribbon, wire, thread, buttons, and beads to create one-of-a kind cards to complement your quilts.

Remembrance
••• Lap Quilt

Remembrance Lap Quilt Finished Size: 45" x 58"	FIRST CUT		SECOND CUT	
	Number of Strips or Pieces	Dimensions	Number of Pieces	Dimensions
Fabric A Block Triangles ⅞ yard each of 2 fabrics	8*	3½" x 42" *cut for each fabric	48*	3½" x 6½"
Fabric B Block Small Triangles ⅝ yard each of 4 fabrics	5*	3½" x 42" *cut for each fabric	48*	3½" squares
Fabric C Sashing ⅝ yard	11	1½" x 42"	31	1½" x 12½"
Fabric D ⅛ yard	1	1½" x 42"	20	1½" squares
Outside Border ½ yard	5	2½" x 42"		
Binding ⅝ yard	6	2¾" x 42"		
Backing - 2⅞ yards Batting - 51" x 64"				

Fabric Requirements and Cutting Instructions

Read all instructions before beginning and use ¼"-wide seam allowances throughout. Read Cutting Strips and Pieces on page 92 prior to cutting fabric.

Getting Started

Nothing is harder for a family than watching a loved one forget their most precious memories. Make this quilt to show your love for them and enjoy the gleam in their eyes when they receive this precious gift. Block measures 12½" square (unfinished). Refer to Accurate Seam Allowance on page 92. Whenever possible use Assembly Line Method on page 92. Press seams in direction of arrows.

Making the Remembrance Block

1. Refer to Quick Corner Triangles on page 92. Making quick corner triangle units, sew two different 3½" Fabric B squares to one 3½" x 6½" Fabric A piece as shown. Press. Make forty-eight matching units.

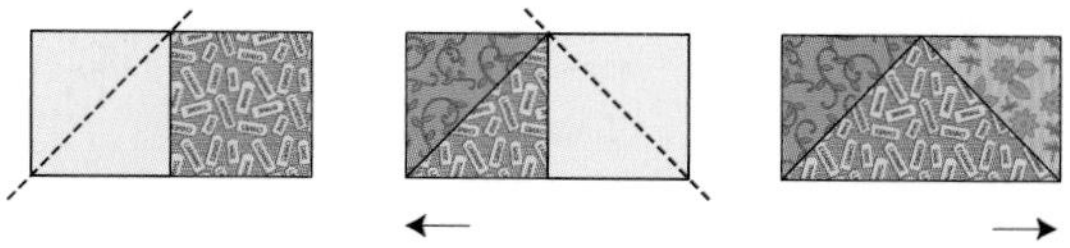

Fabric B = 3½ x 3½
Fabric A = 3½ x 6½
Make 48

2. Making quick corner triangle units, sew two different 3½" Fabric B squares to one 3½" x 6½" Fabric A piece as shown. Press. Make forty-eight matching units.

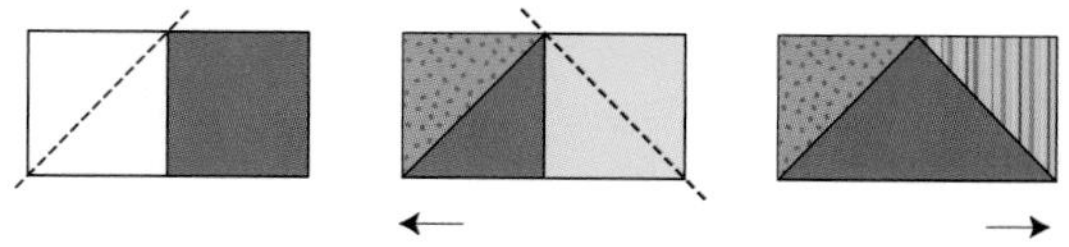

Fabric B = 3½ x 3½
Fabric A = 3½ x 6½
Make 48

3. Sew one unit from step 1 to one unit from step 2 as shown. Press. Make forty-eight.

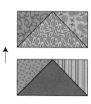

Make 48

4. Sew two units from step 3 together as shown. Press. Make twenty-four.

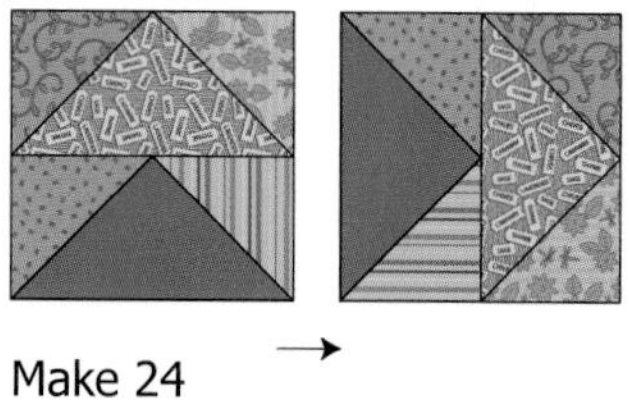

Make 24

This intriguing block creates many interesting patterns in this quilt, making it fun to look at as well as to cuddle under. Make this quilt for an Alzheimer's patient or for a dedicated caregiver who also needs the cozy comfort and cheerful colors of a quilt.

5. Sew two units from step 4 together in pairs as shown. Refer to Twisting Seams on page 92. Press. Make twelve. Remembrance Block measures 12½" square.

Remembrance Block

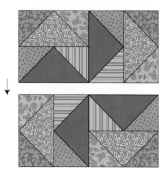

Make 12
Block measures 12½" square

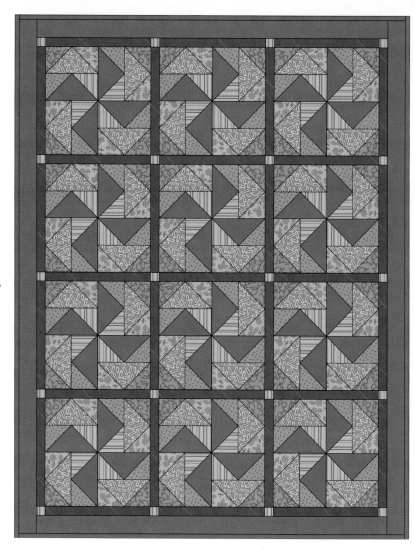

Remembrance Lap Quilt
Finished Size: 45" x 58"

Assembling the Quilt

1. Sew four 1½" Fabric D squares and three 1½" x 12½" Fabric C strips together as shown. Press. Make five rows.

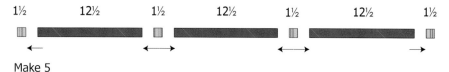

| 1½ | 12½ | 1½ | 12½ | 1½ | 12½ | 1½ |

Make 5

2. Sew four 1½" x 12½" Fabric C strips and three Remembrance Blocks together as shown. Press. Make four rows.

1½   1½   1½   1½

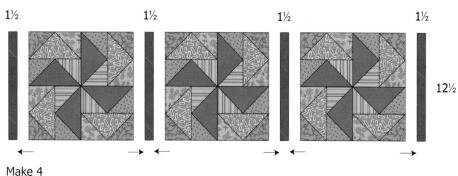

12½

Make 4

3. Referring to photo on page 23 and layout on page 24, arrange and sew together rows from steps 1 and 2. Press.

4. Refer to Adding the Borders on page 94. Sew 2½" x 42" Outside Border strips together end-to-end to make one continuous 2½"-wide Outside Border strip. Measure quilt through center from side to side. Cut two 2½"-wide Outside Border strips to this measurement. Sew to top and bottom of quilt. Press seams toward border.

5. Measure quilt through center from top to bottom including border just added. Cut two 2½"-wide Outside Border strips to this measurement. Sew to sides of quilt. Press.

Layering and Finishing

1. Cut backing crosswise into two equal pieces. Sew pieces together lengthwise to make one 51" x 80" (approximate) backing piece. Press and trim to 51" x 64".

2. Referring to Layering the Quilt on page 94, arrange and baste backing, batting, and top together. Hand or machine quilt as desired.

3. Refer to Binding the Quilt on page 94. Sew 2¾" x 42" binding strips end-to-end to make one continuous 2¾"-wide binding strip. Bind quilt to finish.

Quilters Care
• • • about Alzheimer's Disease

Alzheimer's takes a toll not only on those with the disease but also on families and caregivers who care for those affected by the disease.

The Alzheimer's Art Quilt Initiative was started by a quilter whose mother was affected by the disease. Ami Simms believes it is possible to make a difference - one quilt at a time - and since its founding, this Internet-driven, grassroots, totally volunteer organization has raised more than $290,000 (July 2009) for Alzheimer's research.

The AAQI currently administers two major programs. The first is a nationwide traveling quilt exhibit called "Alzheimer's: Forgetting Piece By Piece." It contains 52 quilts each interpreting Alzheimer's in some way. So far, more than 200,000 people have had the opportunity to see this exhibit.

The second is the "Priority: Alzheimer's Quilts" project, so named for the urgent need for research dollars and the requirement that these quilts must fit into a cardboard USPS priority mailer without folding. They are small works of art no larger than 9 inches by 12 inches, auctioned on the first ten days of each month or sold outright on the Internet or at selected venues across the United States.

Find more information about AAQI at www.alzquilts.org.
For more information about Alzheimer's Disease, check out www.alz.org or www.alzheimer.ca.

Thoughtful Flowers ... Wall Quilt

Thoughtful Flowers Wall Quilt Finished Size: 25" x 26"	FIRST CUT		SECOND CUT	
	Number of Strips or Pieces	Dimensions	Number of Pieces	Dimensions
Background ½ yard	1	16½" x 42"	1	16½" square
Accent Border ⅛ yard	2	1" x 42"	2	1" x 17½"
			2	1" x 16½"
Outside Border ¾ yard	1	24½" x 42"	1	24½" x 5" (Bottom)
			1	24½" x 4" (Top)
			2	4" x 17½" (Sides)
Binding ⅜ yard	4	2¾" x 42"		
Flower Appliqués - Assorted scraps Leaf Appliqués - Assorted scraps Backing - ⅞ yard Batting - 29" x 30" Lightweight Fusible Web - ½ yard				

Fabric Requirements and Cutting Instructions

Read all instructions before beginning and use ¼"-wide seam allowances throughout. Read Cutting Strips and Pieces on page 92 prior to cutting fabric.

Getting Started

This small wall quilt is sure to brighten anyone's day with its gift of flowers that bloom all year long. Refer to Accurate Seam Allowance on page 92.

Making the Quilt

1. Sew 16½" Background square between two 1" x 16½" Accent Border strips. Press seams toward border. Sew this unit between two 1" x 17½" Accent Border strips. Press.

2. Sew unit from step 1 between two 4" x 17½" (sides) Outside Border strips. Press seams toward border. Sew this unit between one 24½" x 4" (top) and one 24½" x 5" (bottom) Outside Border strips. Press.

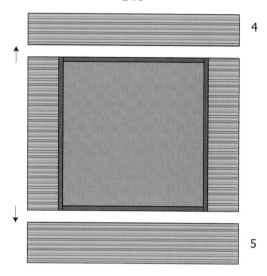

Adding the Appliqués

Refer to appliqué instructions on page 93. Our instructions are for Quick-Fuse Appliqué, but if you prefer hand appliqué, reverse templates and add ¼"-wide seam allowances.

1. Use patterns on pages 28 and 29 to trace flowers and leaves on paper side of fusible web. Use appropriate fabrics to prepare all appliqués for fusing.

2. Refer to photo to position and fuse appliqués to quilt. Finish appliqué edges with machine satin stitch or other decorative stitching as desired.

Layering and Finishing

1. Referring to Layering the Quilt on page 94, arrange and baste backing, batting, and top together. Hand or machine quilt as desired.

2. Refer to Binding the Quilt on page 94. Use 2¾"-wide binding strips to bind quilt.

Create a bright and colorful environment for an Alzheimer's patient or anyone who is housebound. The simple flowers in this design are easy to understand and appreciate and will add cheerful ambiance to any room.

**Thoughtful Flowers
Wall Quilt**

Tracing Line _____
Placement Line _._._._._._._._._.

Flower #1
Make 1

Flower #2
Make 2
(1 with large center,
1 with small center)

Large Leaf
Make 7

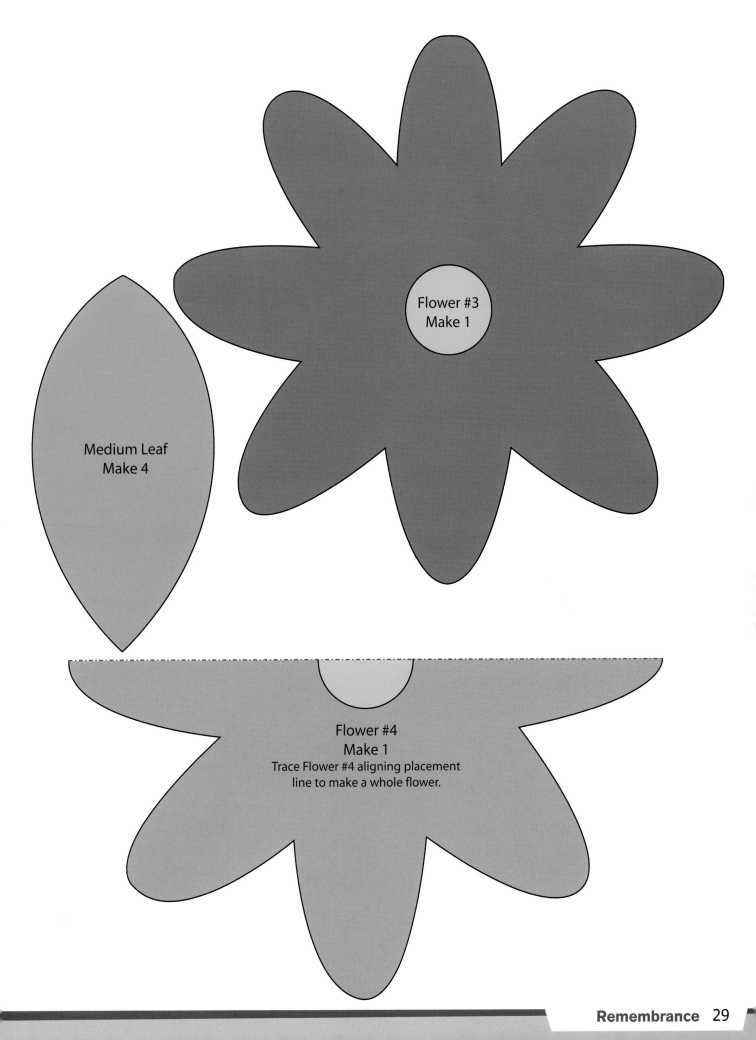

Flower #3
Make 1

Medium Leaf
Make 4

Flower #4
Make 1
Trace Flower #4 aligning placement
line to make a whole flower.

Gratitude
··· Lap Quilt

Gratitude Lap Quilt Finished Size: 51" x 71½"	FIRST CUT		SECOND CUT	
	Number of Strips or Pieces	Dimensions	Number of Pieces	Dimensions
Fabric A Block Center ⅛ yard	1	2½" x 42"	12	2½" squares
Fabric B Block Center ¼ yard	1 1	2½" x 42" 2" x 42"	12 12	2½" squares 2" squares
Fabric C Block First & Fifth Log ⅔ yard	10 4	1½" x 42" 1¼" x 42"	24 24 24 24	1½" x 8" 1½" x 7" 1¼" x 3¼" 1¼" x 2½"
Fabric D Block Second Log ⅓ yard	5	2" x 42"	24 24	2" x 4¾" 2" x 3¼"
Fabric E Block Third Log & Sashing Accents ½ yard	1 7	2" x 42" 1¼" x 42"	17 6 24 24	2" x 1½" 1½" squares 1¼" x 5½" 1¼" x 4¾"
Fabric F Block Fourth Log ⅝ yard	9	2" x 42"	24 24	2" x 7" 2" x 5½"
Fabric G Block Sixth Log ¾ yard	11	2" x 42"	24 24	2" x 9½" 2" x 8"
Fabric H Sashing ⅞ yard	9 6	2" x 42" 1½" x 42"	34 24	2" x 9½" 1½" x 9½"
First Border ⅓ yard	6	1¼" x 42"		
Second Border ⅓ yard	6	1½" x 42"		
Third Border ⅓ yard	6	1½" x 42"		
Outside Border ⅓ yard	6	1½" x 42"		
Binding ⅝ yard	7	2¾" x 42"		
Backing - 3⅓ yards Batting - 59" x 79"				

Fabric Requirements and Cutting Instructions

Read all instructions before beginning and use ¼"-wide seam allowances throughout. Read Cutting Strips and Pieces on page 92 prior to cutting fabric.

Getting Started

This graphic quilt is easy to make using a variation of the traditional Log Cabin block with sashing separating each block. Block measures 9½" square (unfinished). Refer to Accurate Seam Allowance on page 92. Whenever possible use Assembly Line Method on page 92. Press seams in direction of arrows.

Making the Log Cabin Variation Blocks

1. Sew one 2½" Fabric A square to one 1¼" x 2½" Fabric C piece as shown. Press. Sew this unit to one 1½" x 3¼" Fabric C piece. Press. Make twelve.

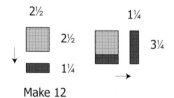

Make 12

2. Sew one unit from step 1 to one 2" x 3¼" Fabric D piece as shown. Press. Sew this unit to one 2" x 4¾" Fabric D piece. Press. Make twelve.

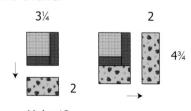

Make 12

Acknowledge a gift of time, talent, food, or support with a quilt that expresses your gratitude. Fabrics build, one upon the other, to create warmth, color, and comfort in this quilt——much the same way kindnesses build upon each other.

3. Sew one unit from step 2 to one 1¼" x 4¾" Fabric E piece as shown. Press. Sew this unit to one 1¼" x 5½" Fabric E piece. Press. Make twelve.

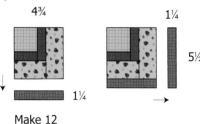

Make 12

4. Sew one unit from step 3 to one 2" x 5½" Fabric F piece as shown. Press. Sew this unit to one 2" x 7" Fabric F piece. Press. Make twelve.

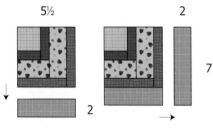

Make 12

5. Sew one unit from step 4 to one 1½" x 7" Fabric C piece as shown. Press. Sew this unit to one 1½" x 8" Fabric C piece. Press. Make twelve.

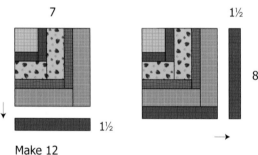

Make 12

6. Sew one unit from step 5 to one 2" x 8" Fabric G piece as shown. Press. Sew this unit to one 2" x 9½" Fabric G piece. Press. Make twelve and label Block 1. Block measures 9½" square.

Block 1

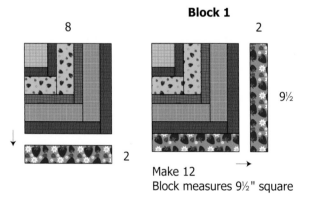

Make 12
Block measures 9½" square

7. Referring to steps 1-6, make twelve blocks substituting 2½" Fabric B squares for Fabric A squares in step 1. Label these Block 2. Block measures 9½" square.

Block 2

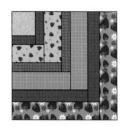

Make 12
Block measures 9½" square

Quilters Care
● ● ● **about saying "Thank you"**

Don't let a good turn go unnoticed! Say thanks in a creative way.

♥ Send a photo that the recipient will enjoy.

♥ Hand-write a note.

♥ Deliver a batch of cupcakes.

♥ Take your best supporter out to breakfast.

♥ Surprise her with flowers or vegetables from your garden.

♥ Add to her fabric stash or craft supplies.

♥ Make him a card (page 21).

♥ Invite her over for coffee or tea.

♥ Help him with something he finds difficult.

♥ Make her favorite dessert.

Assembling the Quilt

1. Arrange and sew together three 2" Fabric B squares, four 2" x 9½" Fabric H strips, and two 1½" x 2" Fabric E pieces as shown. Press. Make four and label these Rows 1, 5, 9, and 13.

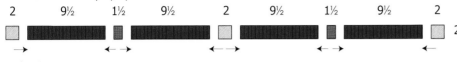

Make 4
Label Rows 1, 5, 9 & 13

2. Arrange and sew together three 1½" x 2" Fabric E pieces, four 1½" x 9½" Fabric H strips, and two 1½" Fabric E squares as shown. Press. Make three and label these Rows 3, 7, and 11.

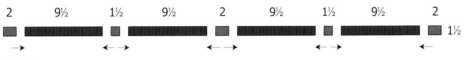

Make 3
Label Rows 3, 7 & 11

3. Arrange and sew together three 2" x 9½" Fabric H strips, two of Block 1, two 1½" x 9½" Fabric H strips, and two of Block 2 as shown. Press and label these Rows 2, 6, and 10.

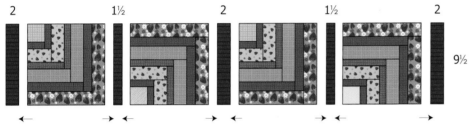

Make 2
Label Rows 2, 6 & 10

4. Arrange and sew together three 2" x 9½" Fabric H strips, two of Block 2, two 1½" x 9½" Fabric H strips, and two of Block 1 as shown. Press and label these Rows 4, 8, and 12.

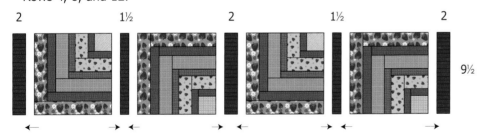

Make 3
Label Rows 4, 8 & 12

5. Referring to photo on page 31, arrange and sew rows from steps 1-4 together. Press. This completes the center of the quilt.

Adding the Borders

1. Refer to Adding the Borders on page 94. Sew 1¼" x 42" First Border strips together end-to-end to make one continuous 1¼"-wide First Border strip. Measure quilt through center from side to side. Cut two 1¼"-wide First Border strips to this measurement. Sew to top and bottom of quilt. Press seams toward border.

2. Measure quilt through center from top to bottom including border just added. Cut two 1¼"-wide First Border strips to this measurement. Sew to sides of quilt. Press.

3. Refer to steps 1 and 2 to join, measure, trim, and sew 1½"-wide Second Border strips, 1½"-wide Third Border strips, and 1½"-wide Outside Border strips to top, bottom, and sides of quilt. Press.

Layering and Finishing

1. Cut backing crosswise into two equal pieces. Sew pieces together lengthwise to make one 60" x 80" (approximate) backing piece. Press.

2. Referring to Layering the Quilt on page 94, arrange and baste backing, batting, and top together. Hand or machine quilt as desired.

3. Refer to Binding the Quilt on page 94. Sew 2¾" x 42" binding strips end-to-end to make one continuous 2¾"-wide binding strip. Bind quilt to finish.

" Too often we underestimate the power of a touch, a smile, a kind word, a listening ear, an honest compliment, or the smallest act of caring, all of which have the potential to turn a life around."

Leo Buscaglia

Heart to Heart
... Lap Quilt

Note: Refer to Cutting Tip on page 36 before cutting fabrics. A ¼ yard can be used instead of Fat Quarters if desired.

Red Heart Lap Quilt Finished Size: 43½" x 55½"	FIRST CUT	
	Number of Strips or Pieces	Dimensions
Fabric A-1 Fat Quarter	1	6½" square
	1	2½" x 6½"
	1	2½" square
Fabric A-2 Fat Quarter	1	6½" square
	3	2½" x 6½"
	1	2½" square
Fabric A-3 ⅛ yard	2	2½" x 6½"
	4	2½" squares
Fabric A-4 Fat Quarter	1	7" square
	3	2½" x 6½"
Fabric A-5 Fat Quarter	1	6½" square
	4	2½" x 6½"
Fabric A-6 Fat Quarter	1	6½" square
	2	2½" x 6½"
	1	2½" square
Fabric A-7 Fat Quarter	1	7" square
	1	6½" square
	5	2½" x 6½"
Fabric B-1 Fat Quarter	1	6½" square
	3	2½" x 6½"
Fabric B-2 Fat Quarter	2	7" squares
	6	2½" x 6½"
	1	2½" square
Fabric B-3 Fat Quarter	2	7" squares
	1	6½" square
	4	2½" x 6½"
	1	2½" square
Fabric B-4 Fat Quarter	1	6½" square
	3	2½" x 6½"
	4	2½" squares
Fabric B-5 Scrap	1	2½" x 6½"
Fabric B-6 Fat Quarter	8	2½" x 6½"
	4	2½" squares
Fabric B-7 ⅛ yard	3	2½" x 6½"
	2	2½" squares
Fabric B-8 ⅛ yard	5	2½" x 6½"

Red Heart Lap Quilt CONTINUED	FIRST CUT	
	Number of Strips or Pieces	Dimensions
Fabric C-1 ⅓ yard	3	7" squares
	2	6½" squares
	3	2½" x 6½"
	3	2½" squares
Fabric C-2 Fat Quarter	1	7" square
	2	6½" squares
	5	2½" x 6½"
	1	2½" square
Fabric C-3 ⅓ yard	2	6½" squares
	7	2½" x 6½"
	5	2½" squares
Fabric C-4 ⅓ yard	1	7" square
	2	6½" squares
	8	2½" x 6½"
	7	2½" squares
Fabric C-5 ⅓ yard	3	7" squares
	6	2½" x 6½"
	2	2½" squares
Fabric C-6 Fat Quarter	1	6½" square
	4	2½" x 6½"
	1	2½" square
Fabric C-7 Fat Quarter	4	6½" squares
	2	2½" x 6½"
	2	2½" squares
Fabric C-8 ⅓ yard	1	7" square
	1	6½" square
	6	2½" x 6½"
	1	2½" square
Fabric C-9 Fat Quarter	1	7" square
	2	6½" squares
	2	2½" x 6½"
	4	2½" squares
Binding** ¼ yard each of 4 fabrics	2*	3½" x 42" *cut for each fabric

Backing - 2⅞ yards
Batting - 50" x 62"
Lightweight Fusible Web - ⅜ yard
**Binding finishes ¾"-wide

Go Red for Women with this eye-catching quilt that typifies the passion, power, and energy of the movement to wipe out heart disease. Simple blocks become a flow of color on this striking quilt while subtle heart appliqués remind us of the challenge. Donate this quilt for a raffle or other fundraising activity or present it to a friend as a heartfelt gift.

Fabric Requirements and Cutting Instructions

Read all instructions before beginning and use ¼"-wide seam allowances throughout. Read Cutting Strips and Pieces on page 92 prior to cutting fabric.

Cutting Tip for Heart to Heart Quilt

Fat Quarters: Cut larger pieces first then the smaller ones.
Fabric with Yardage: Cut a strip by the width of the first size indicated in chart x 42". Cut the number of pieces indicated then cut next size from remaining strip. If needed, cut a strip the width of remaining piece. For example, a piece might need both 7" x 42" strip and 2½" x 42" strip to get the appropriate cuts.

Getting Started

This dramatic red quilt features four different blocks, each measuring 6½" square (unfinished). Because of the color gradation in the quilt, we recommend completely laying out your quilt before assembly. Refer to Accurate Seam Allowance on page 92. Whenever possible use Assembly Line Method on page 92. Press seams in direction of arrows.

Making Stripe Block

This gradated quilt uses different combinations and shades of fabrics to make blocks. Refer to photo on page 35, and diagram on page 37 for fabric selection guide and layout. Sew three different 2½" x 6½" fabric strips together as shown. Press. Make thirty-two in assorted fabric combinations. Block measures 6½" square.

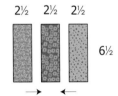

Make 32
(in assorted fabric combinations, according to quilt layout.)
Block measures 6½" square

Making Nine-Patch Block

1. Refer to photo on page 35, and diagram on page 37 for a fabric selection guide. Arrange nine assorted 2½" squares in three rows with three squares each.

2. Sew three 2½" fabric squares together to make a row. Press. Make three rows.

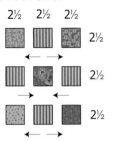

3. Sew rows together as shown. Press. Repeat steps 1 and 2 to make five Nine-Patch Blocks in assorted fabrics. Block measures 6½" square.

Make 5
(in assorted fabric combinations)
Block measures 6½" square

Making Half-Square Triangle Blocks

1. Refer to photo on page 35, and diagram on page 37 for a fabric selection guide. Pair two different 7" squares together.

2. Draw a diagonal line on wrong side of one 7" fabric square. Place marked square and one 7" fabric square right sides together. Sew scant ¼" away from drawn line on both sides to make half-square triangle units as shown. Make eight in assorted fabrics. Cut on drawn line and press. Square to 6½". This will make sixteen half-square triangle units; only eight will be used for this project, one of each combination.

 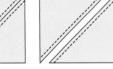

Fabric = 7 x 7
Fabric = 7 x 7
Make 8
(one of each combination)

Square to 6½"
Make 16
Half-square Triangles
(Only 8 will be used in this project, one of each combination.)

Adding the Appliqués

Refer to appliqué instructions on page 93. Our instructions are for Quick-Fuse Appliqué, but if you prefer hand appliqué, add ¼"-wide seam allowances.

1. Use pattern on page 38 to trace six hearts on paper side of fusible web. Use one 6½" square each of Fabrics B-1, B-3, C-1, C-3, C-4, and C-9 to prepare all appliqués for fusing.

2. Referring to photo on page 35, and diagram on page 37, fuse hearts to appropriate blocks. B-3, C-1, and C-4 fabric hearts are fused to Stripe Blocks, B-1 to a Nine-Patch Block, C-3 is fused to 6½" Fabric B-4 square, and C-9 heart is fused to a 6½" Fabric C-2 square.

Note: This quilt uses raw edge appliqué technique. The edges are not finished, but will be sewn down during the quilting process.

Assembling the Quilt

1. Referring to diagram below, arrange all blocks and 6½" fabric squares in nine rows with seven blocks each. Note: lighter shades are at the top of quilt and gradually work down to the darker shades at the bottom.

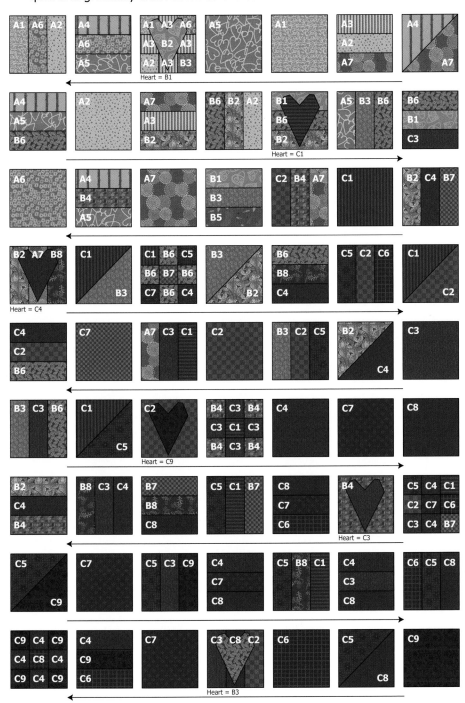

2. Sew blocks into rows noting pressing arrows. Make nine rows.

3. Sew rows together and press.

Layering and Finishing

1. Cut backing crosswise into two equal pieces. Sew pieces together lengthwise to make one 51" x 80" (approximate) backing piece. Press and trim to 51" x 62".

2. Referring to Layering the Quilt on page 94, arrange and baste backing, batting, and top together. Hand or machine quilt as desired. Remember to stitch all heart appliqué edges down during quilting.

3. Refer to Binding the Quilt on page 94. Sew two 3½" x 42" binding strips end-to-end to make one continuous 3½"-wide binding strip. Make four using different fabrics. Bind quilt to finish, sewing the lightest shade on top and the darkest shade on the bottom of the quilt. Note: The binding strip is wider than normal and will measure ¾" finished.

Quilters Care
● ● ● about heart health

The American Heart Association's Go Red for Women and the Heart and Stroke Foundation of Canada's The Heart Truth are programs to help women improve their own cardiovascular health as well as participate in nationwide efforts for heart health.

Here are some things you can do:

♥ **Get Involved.**
Join national and community efforts and become part of the fight against heart disease and stroke.

♥ **Learn about Heart Health.**
On-line heart health quizzes can help you learn more about your risk factors and how to recognize the warning signs of heart disease and stroke.

♥ **Take Control.**
Make lifestyle changes such as quitting smoking, eating a healthier diet and becoming more active to improve your heart health.

♥ **Spread the Message.**
Share information about the risk of heart disease and stroke with friends and family. Volunteer to help with community events.

Find more information and tools to evaluate your risk and take action at these websites:
www.goredforwomen.org
www.thehearttruth.ca

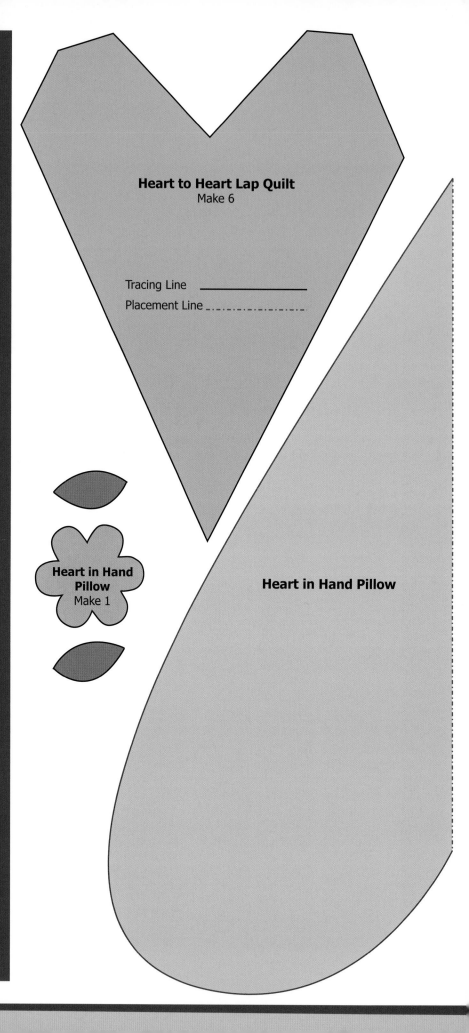

Heart to Heart Lap Quilt
Make 6

Tracing Line _____
Placement Line _ _ _ _ _ _ _ _ _ _ _

Heart in Hand Pillow
Make 1

Heart in Hand Pillow

Heart in Hand
··· Basket

Heart in Hand Basket Finished Size: 7" x 8"	FIRST CUT	
	Number of Strips or Pieces	Dimensions
Heart ⅓ yard (Wool)	2	12" square
Flower Appliqués - Assorted Wool Scraps Interfacing - ⅓ yard Stabilizer - ⅓ yard Embroidery Floss - Pink & Green Polyester Fiberfill Bead - 1 Template Plastic or Pattern Paper Removable Fabric Marker Permanent Marker		

Show a loved one that you care with this gift basket that will brighten a hospital stay or housebound recovery. A handmade wool heart will be a lasting memento of your care while needlework kits, notecards, books, and goodies will provide activities and distractions.

Making the Heart Pillow

1. Referring to Tips for Felting Wool on page 95, felt wool if desired. When dry, interface wool following manufacturer's instructions.

2. Hand or machine embroider "FRIEND" on 12" heart square. We used the Bernina® artista 780 using the Swiss Block font with 4mm spacing.

3. To prepare heart pattern, trace ½ heart pattern and a reversed (mirror image) ½ heart pattern, aligning sections along placement line to make a complete pattern.

4. Referring to photo and using removable fabric marker, trace heart shape onto embroidered 12" heart square, centering pattern over "FRIEND".

5. Use pattern on page 38 to trace one small flower and two leaves on paper side of fusible web. Use appropriate fabrics to prepare all appliqués for fusing.

6. Refer to photo to position and fuse appliqués to heart, allowing for ¼" seam allowance on all sides when placing appliqués.

7. Refer to Embroidery Guide on page 95. Use a stem stitch and three strands of green embroidery floss to embroider a stem for flower.

8. Using a large running stitch and six strands of pink embroidery floss, stitch around heart shape approximately ½" in from drawn line.

9. Cut out heart shape on traced line. Layer heart and 12" heart square right sides together. Using ¼"-wide seam, stitch around entire shape. Trim backing piece to match heart shape.

10. Cut a slit in the center of backing piece being careful not to cut front fabric piece. Clip curves and turn piece right side out. Stuff heart with polyester fiberfill to desired fullness. Whipstitch opening closed.

11. Iron fusible web to a piece of scrap fabric. Using pinking shears or wavy blade rotary cutter, cut out a 2" x 3" rectangle from fabric scrap. Using a permanent marker, sign and date or write a personal message of support on the rectangle. Fuse to back of heart covering whip stitches.

Blankie for Baby
··· Crib Quilt

Blankie for Baby Crib Quilt Finished Size: 41½" x 48½"	FIRST CUT		SECOND CUT	
	Number of Strips or Pieces	Dimensions	Number of Pieces	Dimensions
Fabric A Block 1 Center ½ yard	2	6" x 42"	10	6" squares
Fabric B Block 1 Border ⅜ yard	8	1¼" x 42"	20 20	1¼" x 7½" 1¼" x 6"
Fabric C Block 2 ⅓ yard	2	4" x 42"		
Fabric D Block 2 ⅓ yard	2	4" x 42"		
Fabric E Block 3 Center ½ yard	2	7½" x 42"	10	7½" squares
Fabric F Block 3 Accent ½ yard	4	4" x 42"	40	4" squares
First Border ⅙ yard	4	1" x 42"		
Second Border ¼ yard	5	1¼" x 42"		
Outside Border ⅓ yard	5	2" x 42"		
Binding ½ yard	5	2¾" x 42"		
Backing - 2⅝ yards Batting - 47" x 54"				

Fabric Requirements and Cutting Instructions

Read all instructions before beginning and use ¼"-wide seam allowances throughout. Read Cutting Strips and Pieces on page 92 prior to cutting fabric.

Getting Started

This crib quilt is a play of squares using three different block patterns. Each block measures 7½" square (unfinished). Refer to Accurate Seam Allowance on page 92. Whenever possible use Assembly Line Method on page 92. Press seams in direction of arrows.

Making Block 1

Sew one 6" Fabric A square between two 1¼" x 6" Fabric B pieces as shown. Press. Sew this unit between two 1¼" x 7½" Fabric B pieces. Press. Make ten and label Block 1. Block measures 7½" square.

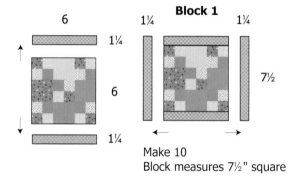

Make 10
Block measures 7½" square

Making Block 2

1. Sew together lengthwise one 4" x 42" Fabric C strip and one 4" x 42" Fabric D strip to make a strip set. Press seam toward Fabric C. Make two. Cut strip set into twenty 4"-wide segments as shown.

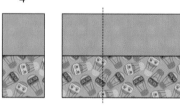

Make 2
Cut 20 segments

2. Sew two units from step 1 together as shown. Press. Make ten and label Block 2. Block measures 7½" square.

Block 2

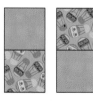

Make 10
Block measures 7½" square

He'll find lots to look at, dream about, and imagine when this colorful quilt becomes his safe haven. We chose jungle prints and a word pattern for this easy-to-make crib quilt that will serve him well for years to come.

Blankie for Baby Crib Quilt
Finished Size: 41½" x 48½"

Making Block 3

Refer to Quick Corner Triangles on page 92. Making quick corner triangle units, sew four 4" Fabric F squares to one 7½" Fabric E square as shown. Press. Make ten and label Block 3. Block measures 7½" square.

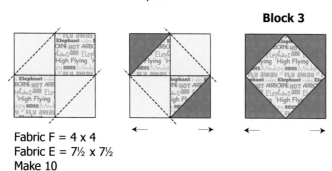

Block 3

Fabric F = 4 x 4
Fabric E = 7½ x 7½
Make 10
Block measures 7½" square

Assembling the Quilt

1. Referring to photo on page 41 and layout, arrange and sew together six rows with five blocks each. Press seams in opposite direction from row to row.

2. Arrange and sew rows together from step 1. Press.

3. Refer to Adding the Borders on page 94. Measure quilt through center from side to side. Cut two 1"-wide First Border strips to this measurement. Sew to top and bottom of quilt. Press seams toward border.

4. Sew remaining strips from step 3 and 1" x 42" First Border strips together end-to-end to make one continuous 1"-wide First Border strip. Measure quilt through center from top to bottom including border just added. Cut two 1"-wide First Border strips to this measurement. Sew to sides of quilt. Press.

5. Refer to steps 1 and 2 to join, measure, trim, and sew 1¼"-wide Second Border and 2"-wide Outside Border strips to top, bottom, and sides of quilt. Press.

Layering and Finishing

1. Cut backing crosswise into two equal pieces. Sew pieces together lengthwise to make one 47" x 80" (approximate) backing piece. Press and trim to 47" x 54".

2. Referring to Layering the Quilt on page 94, arrange and baste backing, batting, and top together. Hand or machine quilt as desired.

3. Refer to Binding the Quilt on page 94. Sew 2¾" x 42" binding strips end-to-end to make one continuous 2¾"-wide binding strip. Bind quilt to finish.

Blankie for Baby
···Small Quilt

This quilt is a smaller size for a preemie or baby in the NICU. Pretty colors and eye-catching prints will help her see the coming joys.

Pink Blankie for Baby Small Quilt Finished Size: 36" x 36"	FIRST CUT		SECOND CUT	
	Number of Strips or Pieces	Dimensions	Number of Pieces	Dimensions
Fabric A Block 1 Center ½ yard	2	6" x 42"	8	6" squares
Fabric B Block 1 Border ⅓ yard	7	1¼" x 42"	16 16	1¼" x 7½" 1¼" x 6"
Fabric C Block 2 ⅓ yard	2	4" x 42"		
Fabric D Block 2 ⅓ yard	2	4" x 42"		
Fabric E Block 3 Center ½ yard	2	7½" x 42"	8	7½" squares
Fabric F Block 3 Accent ½ yard	4	4" x 42"	32	4" squares
Binding ⅜ yard	4	2¾" x 42"		
Backing - 1⅛ yards Batting - 40" x 40"				

2. Arrange and sew together two of Block 3, two of Block 2 and one of Block 1. Press odd row seams in one direction and even row seams in opposite directions. Make two and label Rows 1 and 5.

3. Arrange and sew together two of Block 2, two of Block 1 and one of Block 3. Press. Make two and label Rows 2 and 4.

4. Arrange and sew together two of Block 1, two of Block 3 and one of Block 2. Press and label Row 3.

5. Sew rows from steps 2-4 together. Press.

Layering and Finishing

1. Referring to Layering the Quilt on page 94, arrange and baste backing, batting, and top together. Hand or machine quilt as desired.

2. Refer to Binding the Quilt on page 94. Use 2¾"-wide Binding strips to bind quilt.

Making the Quilt

For all of the following steps refer to photo to arrange and sew blocks together.

1. Refer to Blankie for Baby Crib Quilt on pages 40-42 to make eight of Block 1, nine of Block 2, and 8 of Block 3. Blocks measure 7½" square.

Block 1

Make 8

Block 2

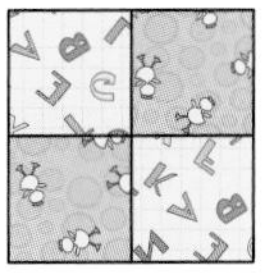

Make 9

Block 3

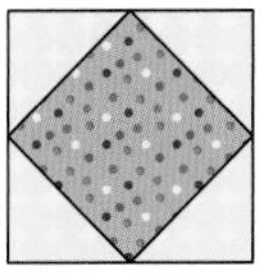

Make 8

Blocks measure 7½" square

ELEPHANT
... Crib Quilt

Elephant Crib Quilt Finished Size: 38" x 46"	FIRST CUT		SECOND CUT	
	Number of Strips or Pieces	Dimensions	Number of Pieces	Dimensions
Fabric A Background ⅞ yard	3	8½" x 42"	10	8½" squares
Fabric B Elephant Background ⅞ yard	3	8½" x 42"	10	8½" squares
Elephant Appliqués ⅛ yard each of 3 light fabrics				
First Border ¼ yard	4	1½" x 42"		
Outside Border ⅓ yard	5	2" x 42"		
Binding ½ yard	5	2¾" x 42"		
Backing - 1½ yards (Fabric needs to be at least 44"-wide or 2½ yards pieced) Batting - 44" x 52" Lightweight Fusible Web - ⅔ yard Embroidery Floss - Dark blue				

Fabric Requirements and Cutting Instructions

Read all instructions before beginning and use ¼"-wide seam allowances throughout. Read Cutting Strips and Pieces on page 92 prior to cutting fabric.

Getting Started

These elephants march in a parade in both our boy and girl versions of this quilt. The boy's quilt uses two background fabrics and three different appliqué elephant fabrics, while the girl's version is smaller and uses two different appliqué elephant fabrics. Make your quilt using one of our versions or make a scrappy quilt using a variety of fabrics from your stash. Each block measures 8½" square (unfinished). Refer to Accurate Seam Allowance on page 92. Whenever possible use Assembly Line Method on page 92. Press seams in direction of arrows.

Making the Boy's Elephant Quilt

1. Sew two 8½" Fabric A squares and two 8½" Fabric B squares together as shown. Press. Make three and label Rows 1, 3, and 5.

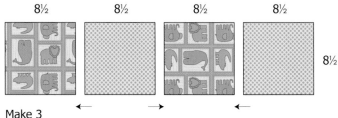

Make 3
Label Rows 1, 3, & 5

2. Sew two 8½" Fabric B squares and two 8½" Fabric A squares together as shown. Press. Make two and label Rows 2 and 4.

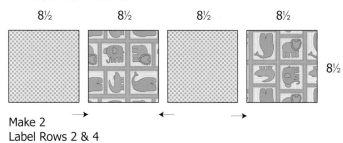

Make 2
Label Rows 2 & 4

3. Referring to photo and layout on page 46, arrange and sew rows together from step 1 and 2. Press.

Adding the Appliqués

Refer to appliqué instructions on page 93. Our instructions are for Quick-Fuse Appliqué, but if you prefer hand appliqué, and add ¼"-wide seam allowances.

1. Use patterns on page 46 to trace a total of ten elephants on paper side of fusible web. Pattern states quantity needed for each direction. Use appropriate fabrics to prepare all appliqués for fusing.

2. Refer to photo and layout on page 46 to position and fuse appliqués to quilt. Finish appliqué edges with machine satin stitch or other decorative stitching as desired.

3. Machine satin stitch tail and around tail appliqué piece. Refer to Embroidery Stitch Guide on page 95. Using three strands of embroidery floss, stitch a French Knot for each elephant's eye.

Sweet little elephants will be at baby's side providing the snuggly comfort and sheltering warmth of a handmade quilt whenever he needs an extra cuddle. Quick-Fuse Applique makes short work of the elephant herd. Showcase a Noah's Ark or animal print for alternating blocks.

Adding the Borders

1. Refer to Adding the Borders on page 94. Measure quilt through center from side to side. Cut two 1½"-wide First Border strips to this measurement. Sew to top and bottom of quilt. Press seams toward border.

2. Sew remaining strips from step 1 and 1½" x 42" First Border strips together end-to-end to make one continuous 1½"-wide First Border strip. Measure quilt through center from top to bottom including border just added. Cut two 1½"-wide First Border strips to this measurement. Sew to sides of quilt. Press.

3. Refer to steps 1 and 2 to measure, trim, and sew 2"-wide Outside Border strips to top, bottom, and sides of quilt. Press.

Layering and Finishing

1. Referring to Layering the Quilt on page 94, arrange and baste backing, batting, and top together. Hand or machine quilt as desired.

2. Refer to Binding the Quilt on page 94. Sew 2¾" x 42" binding strips end-to-end to make one continuous 2¾"-wide binding strip. Bind quilt to finish.

Elephant Crib Quilt
Finished Size: 38" x 46"

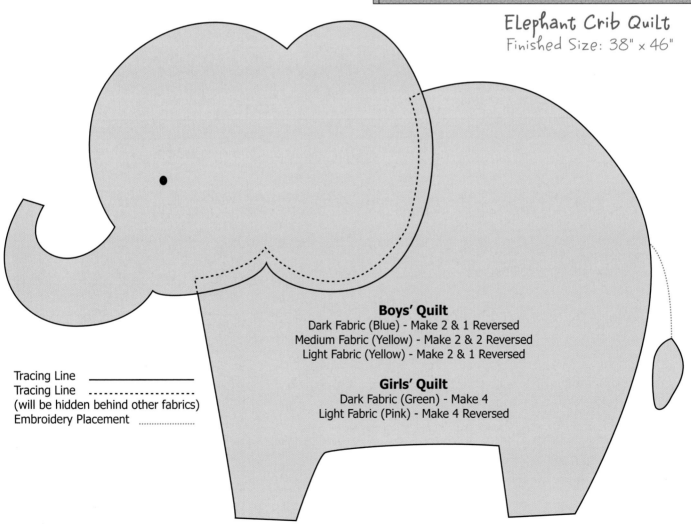

Tracing Line ——————————
Tracing Line ------------------
(will be hidden behind other fabrics)
Embroidery Placement ....

Boys' Quilt
Dark Fabric (Blue) - Make 2 & 1 Reversed
Medium Fabric (Yellow) - Make 2 & 2 Reversed
Light Fabric (Yellow) - Make 2 & 1 Reversed

Girls' Quilt
Dark Fabric (Green) - Make 4
Light Fabric (Pink) - Make 4 Reversed

Quilters Care
about all children

No one needs a security blanket more than a child in a stressful situation and quilters meet this challenge by donating quilts of all sizes to the most vulnerable. Quilters know that a special, completely-his-own, quilt can help a child through any trauma including everyday growing up!

Helping Locally

There are many opportunities to donate quilts to children in need in your own community.
• Children going into foster care.
• Battered Women/Children Refuges.
• Hospitals: Neonatal Intensive Care Units; pediatric oncology and other children's wards; Shriner's programs. Contact your local hospital first to check on size and material requirements, especially for NICU quilts.
• Check with your local quilt guild for existing programs in which you can participate.
A wide variety of national and regional organizations assist quilters in distributing quilts to children in need. Check online for organizations that focus on your particular interest.

Project Linus:

With hundreds of local chapters and thousands of volunteers across the United States, Project Linus has distributed over 3 million blankets to children in need since 1995. The Project Linus mission is to provide love, a sense of security, warmth and comfort to children who are seriously ill, traumatized, or otherwise in need through the gifts of new, handmade quilts and afghans, lovingly created by volunteers. Check their website (www.projectlinus.com) for a chapter near you.

Quilts for Kids:

This charitable organization transforms discontinued and unwanted fabrics into quilts that comfort children with life-threatening illnesses as well as children of abuse. This international organization has more than 50 sister chapters and has distributed tens of thousands of quilts worldwide. Check their website (www.quiltsforkids.org) for information and a chapter near you.

"When I approach a child
He inspires in me two sentiments:
Tenderness for what he is,
And respect for what he may become."

Robert F Kennedy

ELEPHANT Square Quilt

Two by two, pink and green elephants will brighten the scene for any little girl!

Elephant Square Quilt Finished Size: 36" x 36"	FIRST CUT		SECOND CUT	
	Number of Strips or Pieces	Dimensions	Number of Pieces	Dimensions
Fabric A Background ⅝ yard	2	8½" x 42"	8	8½" squares
Fabric B Elephant Background ⅝ yard	2	8½" x 42"	8	8½" squares
Elephant Appliqués ⅙ yard each of 2 light fabrics				
Border ⅓ yard	4	2" x 42"		
Binding ⅜ yard	4	2¾" x 42"		
Backing - 1⅙ yards Batting - 42" x 42" Lightweight Fusible Web - ⅔ yard Embroidery Floss - Dark blue				

Making the Girl's Elephant Quilt

1. Sew two 8½" Fabric A squares and two 8½" Fabric B squares together as shown. Press. Make two and label Rows 1, and 3.

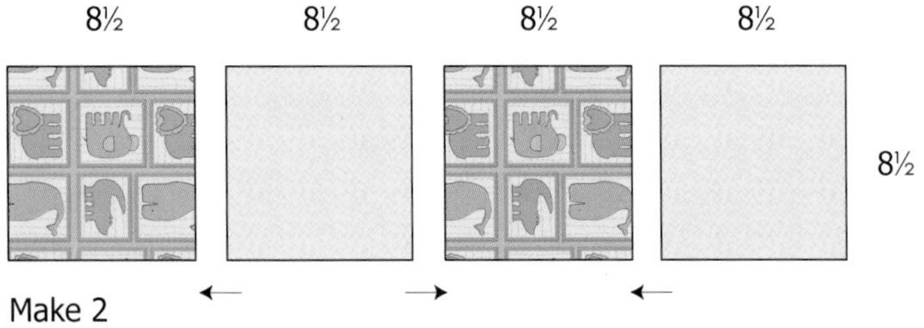

Make 2
Label Rows 1, & 3

2. Sew two 8½" Fabric B squares and two 8½" Fabric A squares together as shown. Press. Make two and label Rows 2 and 4.

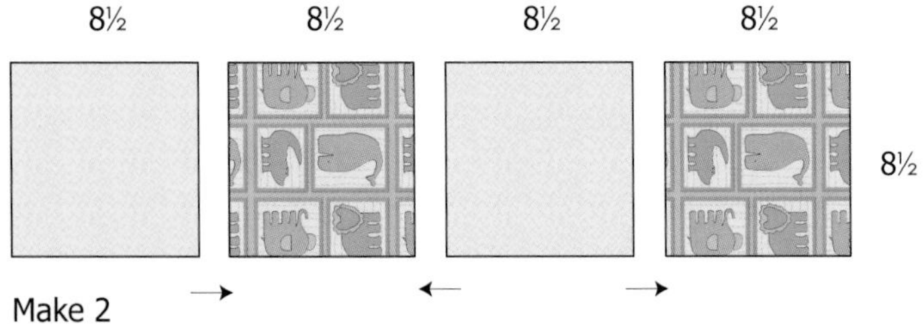

Make 2
Label Rows 2 & 4

3. Referring to photo and layout below, arrange and sew rows together from step 1 and 2. Press.

4. Refer to boy's quilt instructions Adding the Appliqués on page 44 to add eight elephants to quilt (Four and four reversed).

5. Refer to Adding the Borders on page 94. Measure quilt through center from side to side. Cut two 2"-wide First Border strips to this measurement. Sew to top and bottom of quilt. Press seams toward border.

6. Measure quilt through center from top to bottom including border just added. Cut two 2"-wide First Border strips to this measurement. Sew to sides of quilt. Press.

Layering and Finishing

1. Referring to Layering the Quilt on page 94, arrange and baste backing, batting, and top together. Hand or machine quilt as desired.

2. Refer to Binding the Quilt on page 94. Use 2¾"-wide Binding strips to bind quilt.

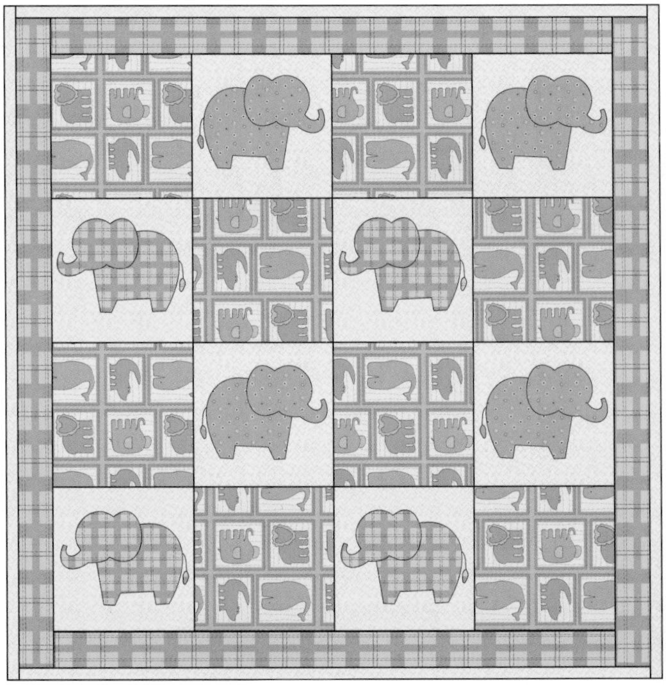

Elephant Square Quilt
Finished Size: 36" x 36"

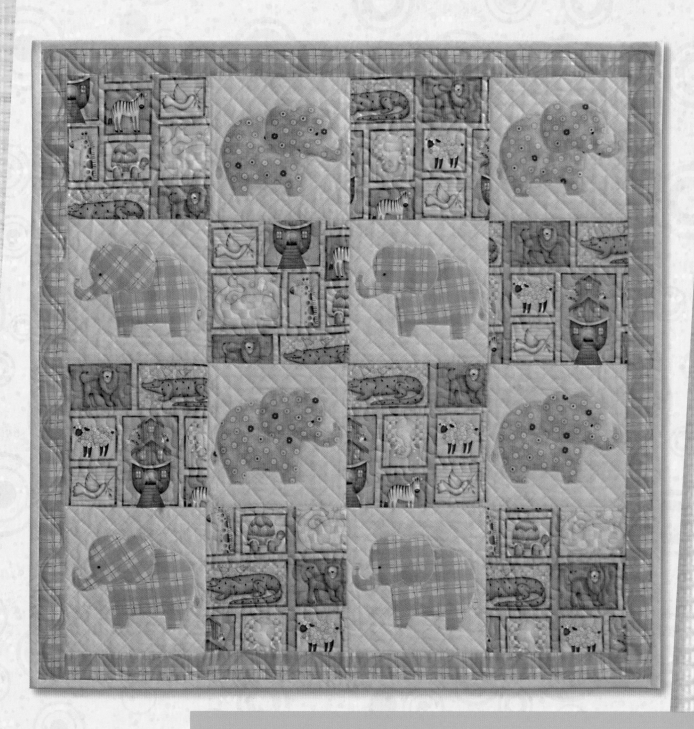

Pink and green elephants, oh my! Any baby girl and her parents would love this totally sweet little quilt - especially a family that needs extra comfort because their baby is in a Neonatal Intensive Care Unit! This 36″ x 36″ quilt is just right to provide a colorful covering for an isolette to block out the light and for the family to use to take home their tiny little girl.

Planet Green ··· Lap Quilt

Planet Green Lap Quilt Finished Size: 51" x 65"	FIRST CUT	
	Number of Strips or Pieces	Dimensions
Fabric A ½ yard	3	4½" x 42"
Fabric B ⅜ yard	2	5½" x 42"
Fabric C ¼ yard	2	3" x 42"
Fabric D ⅜ yard	2	5½" x 42"
Fabric E ¼ yard	2	3" x 42"
Fabric F ⅜ yard*	2	5½" x 42"
First Border ⅓ yard	5	1½" x 42"
Outside Border 1 yard	6	5½" x 42"
Binding ⅝ yard	7	2¾" x 42"
Backing - 3⅙ yards Batting - 57" x 71" Appliqué Leaves - ⅛ yards (Each of four fabrics) Appliqué Circles - Assorted Scraps Lightweight Fusible Web - 1 yard *1⅙ yards needed if stripe runs parallel with selvage		

Fabric Requirements and Cutting Instructions

Read all instructions before beginning and use ¼"-wide seam allowances throughout. Read Cutting Strips and Pieces on page 92 prior to cutting fabric.

Getting Started

This quilt features strips of six different earthy, rich-colored fabrics and a border scattered with appliquéd leaves and circles. Refer to Accurate Seam Allowance on page 92. Whenever possible use Assembly Line Method on page 92. Press seams in direction of arrows.

Assembling the Quilt

1. Arrange and sew together three 4½" x 42" Fabric A strips, two 5½" x 42" Fabric B strips, two 3" x 42" Fabric C strips, two 5½" x 42" Fabric D strips, two 3" x 42" Fabric E strips, and two 5½" x 42" Fabric F strips as shown. Press. Trim unit to measure 38½" x 52½".

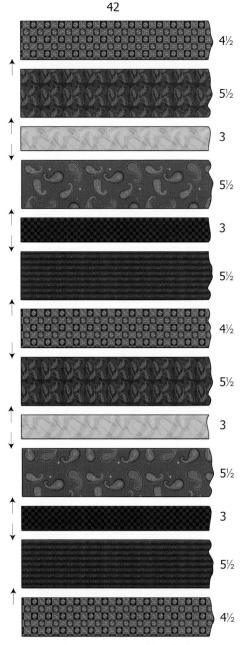

Trim unit to measure 38½ x 52½

Show your commitment to a healthy environment by turning down the thermostat and using this quilt to snuggle up in during those cold winter months. If possible, use leftover strips from your fabric stash and trade with other quilters to get a variety of greens for the leaves.

2. Measure quilt through center from side to side. Cut two 1½" x 42" First Border strips to this measurement. Sew to top and bottom of quilt. Press seams toward border.

3. Refer to Adding the Borders on page 94. Sew 1½" x 42" First Border strips together end-to-end to make one continuous 1½"-wide First Border strip. Measure quilt through center from top to bottom including border just added. Cut two 1½"-wide First Border strips to this measurement. Sew to sides of quilt. Press.

4. Refer to steps 1 and 2 to join, measure, trim, and sew 5½"-wide Outside Border strips to top, bottom, and sides of quilt. Press.

Adding the Appliqués

Refer to appliqué instructions on page 93. Our instructions are for Quick-Fuse Appliqué, but if you prefer hand appliqué, add ¼"-wide seam allowances.

1. Use patterns on pages 55 to trace thirty-two leaves and eight circles on paper side of fusible web. Use appropriate fabrics to prepare all appliqués for fusing.

2. Refer to photo on page 51 to position and fuse appliqués to quilt. Finish appliqué edges with machine satin stitch or other decorative stitching as desired.

Layering and Finishing

1. Cut backing crosswise into two equal pieces. Sew pieces together lengthwise to make one 57" x 80" (approximate) backing piece. Press.

2. Referring to Layering the Quilt on page 94, arrange and baste backing, batting, and top together. Hand or machine quilt as desired.

3. Refer to Binding the Quilt on page 94. Sew 2¾" x 42" binding strips end-to-end to make one continuous 2¾"-wide binding strip. Bind quilt to finish.

> "Humankind has not woven the web of life. We are but one thread within it. Whatever we do to the web, we do to ourselves. All things are bound together. All things connect."
>
> Chief Seattle, 1855

Quilters Care
● ● ● about the planet

Five easy ways to "go green"

1. Bag it. Bring your own reusable bags (Living Green Tote page 56) every time you go shopping. Currently, in order to fill the demand for shopping bags, we use 14 million trees for paper bags and 12 million barrels of oil for plastic bags each year.

2. Conserve it. Electricity, that is. Turn off lights and devices when not in use; open the blinds and let natural light in; wash laundry with cold water; line dry your linens; use compact florescent bulbs to reduce energy use. Check with your local utility about renewable energy programs.

3. Eat it. Shop local farmers markets for seasonal locally grown produce that isn't packaged, processed, and shipped. Good for you, good for the local economy, and good for the environment.

4. Don't Buy it. Drink water from the tap rather than buying single-use bottled water. Bottling water requires energy to produce, store, and transport the product. Buy a reusable bottle to fill from your tap.

5. Save it. Any time we walk, ride a bike, or use public transportation we reduce carbon dioxide and emissions created by driving a gas-powered car. If you need to drive, do all your errands at the same time to reduce the number of trips to and from your house.

Helpful websites:
www.planetgreen.discovery.com;
www.thedailygreen.com

Growing Green
...Wall Quilt

This contemporary wall quilt is a great way to show your personal commitment to leaving a greener footprint on the earth. Rich earth colors, symbolic leaves and sunflowers, and recycled buttons will remind you to reduce, reuse, and recycle.

Growing Green
Wall Quilt
Finished Size: 38" x 54"

Fabric Requirements and Cutting Instructions

Read all instructions before beginning and use ¼"-wide seam allowances throughout. Read Cutting Strips and Pieces on page 92 prior to cutting fabric. Cutting chart is on page 54.

Getting Started

This quilt features a very simple block design. Assorted fabric combinations become our canvas for appliquéd flowers and leaves. Block measures 9" x 25½" (unfinished). Refer to Accurate Seam Allowance on page 92. Whenever possible use Assembly Line Method on page 92. Press seams in direction of arrows.

Adding the Appliqués

Refer to appliqué instructions on page 93 and Mistyfuse™ on page 94. Our instructions are for Quick-Fuse Appliqué, but if you prefer hand appliqué, add ¼"-wide seam allowances. Sometimes when finishing the edges of several appliqué pieces by machine the fabric can shrink slightly. We fused the appliqués to a larger piece of fabric, finished the edges by machine, then cut to size indicated.

1. Use patterns on pages 55 and 95 to trace sixty-four leaves and eight of each size circle 6", 3½", and 2" on paper side of fusible web or freezer paper. Use appropriate fabrics to prepare all appliqués for fusing.

2. Refer to photo (noting direction of leaves) to position and fuse four leaf appliqués to each 6" x 18" Fabric A, B, C, D, E, F, and G strips. Note: Fuse appliqués on an angle and at least 1" away from all edges. Finish appliqué edges with machine satin stitch or other decorative stitching as desired.

Growing Green Wall Quilt Finished Size: 38" x 54"	FIRST CUT		SECOND CUT	
	Number of Strips or Pieces	Dimensions	Number of Pieces	Dimensions
Fabric A — Background — ½ yard	1 1	10" x 42" 6" x 42"	1 3	10" square 6" x 18"
Fabric B — Background — ⅝ yard*	1	18" x 42"* *For directional fabric, the size listed first runs parallel to the selvage.	1 2	10" square 18" x 6"
Fabric C — Background — ⅓ yard	1	10" x 42"	2 1	10" square 6" x 18"
Fabric D — Background — ½ yard	1 1	10" x 42" 6" x 42"	1 3	10" square 6" x 18"
Fabric E — Background — ½ yard	1 1	10" x 42" 6" x 42"	1 3	10" square 6" x 18"
Fabric F — Background — ½ yard	1 1	10" x 42" 6" x 42	1 2	10" square 6" x 18"
Fabric G — Background — ½ yard	1 1	10" x 42" 6" x 42"	1 2	10" square 6" x 18"
First Border — ¼ yard	5	1" x 42"		
Outside Border — ⅓ yard	5	1½" x 42"		
Binding — ½ yard	5	2¾" x 42"		

Backing - 1⅔ yards
(Fabric needs to be at least 44"-wide or 2½ yards pieced)
Batting - 44" x 60"
Leaf Appliqués - ¼ yard each of four fabrics
6" Circle Appliqués - ¼ yard each of four fabrics
3½" Circle Appliqués - Assorted scraps
2" Circle Appliqués - Assorted scraps
Flower Petal Appliqués - ⅛ yard each of four fabrics
Lightweight Fusible Web or Mistyfuse™ - 3 yards
Heavyweight Fusible Web - ½ yard
Buttons - 8 Assorted

3. Cut one flower petal fabric piece into two 3½" x 18" strips. Fuse heavyweight fusible web on the wrong side of one of these strips. Fuse this piece to the matching fabric strip, wrong sides together. Cut strip into twenty-four 1" x 1¼" pieces. Repeat step to make ninety-six petals from four different fabrics.

4. Refer to photo on page 53 to arrange twelve flower petals and one 6" circle to the center of each 10" Fabric A, B, C, D, E, and F square, making sure to keep all appliqués at least ¾" away from all edges. Flower petals extend slightly under circle piece. Fuse in place. Arrange and fuse 3½" and 2" circles to flower. Repeat step for remaining squares. Finish circle edges with machine satin stitch or other decorative stitching as desired, flower petals will remain dimensional.

5. Trim all 6" x 18" appliqué strips to 4¾" x 17" strips and trim 10" appliqué squares to 9" squares making sure appliqués are centered in the piece.

Assembling the Quilt

1. Refer to photo on page 53 to arrange all appliqué units into rows with the leaves pointing in the correct direction.

2. Sew two 4¾" x 17" leaf units together as shown. Make eight, in assorted Fabric A, B, C, D, E, F, and G combinations.

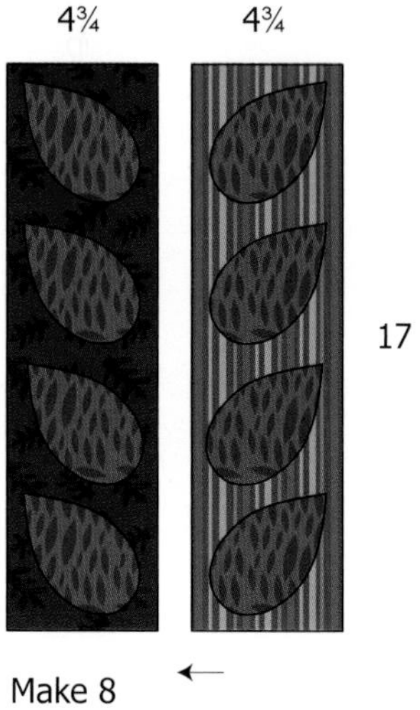

4¾   4¾

17

Make 8
(in assorted combinations)

3. Sew one 9" flower unit to one leaf unit from step 1 as shown. Press. Make eight, four of each variation. Block measures 9" x 25½".

9   9

9

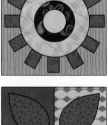
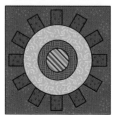

Make 4
(in assorted combinations)
Block measures 9" x 25½"

Make 4
(in assorted combinations)
Block measures 9" x 25½"

4. Refer to photo on page 53 to arrange and sew together two rows with four blocks each. Press seams in opposite directions.

5. Sew rows together. Press.

Adding the Borders

1. Refer to Adding the Borders on page 94. Measure quilt through center from side to side. Cut two 1"-wide First Border strips to this measurement. Sew to top and bottom of quilt. Press seams toward border.

2. Sew 1" x 42" First Border strips together end-to-end to make one continuous 1"-wide First Border strip. Measure quilt through center from top to bottom including border just added. Cut two 1"-wide First Border strips to this measurement. Sew to sides of quilt. Press.

3. Refer to steps 1 and 2 to join, measure, trim, and sew 1½"-wide Outside Border strips to top, bottom, and sides of quilt. Press.

Layering and Finishing

1. Referring to Layering the Quilt on page 94, arrange and baste backing, batting, and top together. Hand or machine quilt as desired.

2. Refer to Binding the Quilt on page 94. Sew 2¾" x 42" binding strips end-to-end to make one continuous 2¾"-wide binding strip. Bind quilt to finish.

3. Sew buttons to center of each flower and add any additional embellishments as desired.

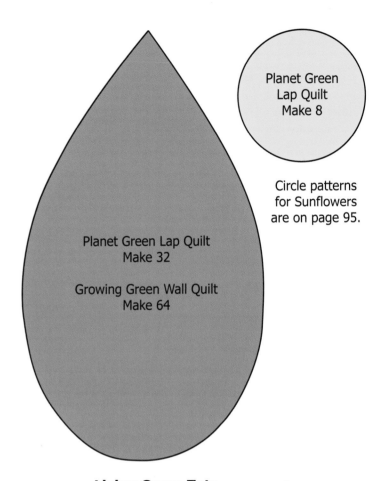

Planet Green
Lap Quilt
Make 8

Circle patterns for Sunflowers are on page 95.

Planet Green Lap Quilt
Make 32

Growing Green Wall Quilt
Make 64

Living Green Tote

Pattern is reversed for use with Quick-Fuse Appliqué (page 93)

Tracing Line _____
Tracing Line - - - - - - - - - - - - - - - - -
(will be hidden behind other fabrics)

Getting Started

Be stylish as well as practical by carrying your groceries home in this fashionable trend-setting tote. Read all instructions before beginning this project. Note this project uses both ½"-wide and ¼"-wide seam allowances. Press seams in direction of arrows.

Making the Tote

1. Using a ¼"-wide seam allowance, sew together one 3½" x 42" Fabric A strip, one 1½" x 42" Fabric B strip, one 9½" x 42" Fabric C strip, and one 8½" x 42" Fabric D strip as shown. Press.

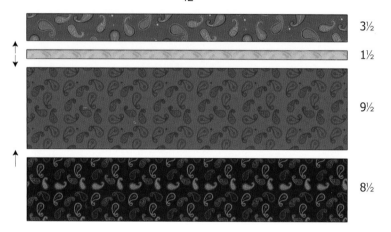

42

3½

1½

9½

8½

2. Place unit from step 1 on 24" x 46" batting and backing pieces and quilt as desired. Trim batting and backing even with tote edges.

3. Cut unit from step 2 into two 20½" x 21" pieces. Referring to diagram to the right and using removable fabric marker, draw handle placement lines 4¾" from each side and 1" toward center from this mark. Center should measure 9".

4. Refer to appliqué instructions on page 93. Our instructions are for Quick-Fuse Appliqué, but if you prefer hand appliqué, reverse templates and add ¼"-wide seam allowances. Use patterns on page 55 to trace bird, branch and leaves on paper side of fusible web. Use appropriate fabrics to prepare all appliqués for fusing.

5. Refer to photo on page 57 and diagram to the right, to position and fuse appliqués to unit from step 3. Finish appliqué edges with machine satin stitch or other decorative stitching as desired. Sew bead for bird's eye.

Living Green Tote Finished Size: 18" x 19"	FIRST CUT	
	Number of Strips or Pieces	Dimensions
Fabric A Top Strip & Lining ¾ yard*	2 1	20½" x 21½" 3½" x 42" *Fabric needs to be at least 44"-wide
Fabric B Accent Strip ⅛ yard	1	1½" x 42"
Fabric C Middle Strip ⅓ yard	1	9½" x 42"
Fabric D Bottom Strip ⅓ yard	1	8½" x 42"
Fabric E Handles ½ yard	3	4½" x 42"
Appliqués - Assorted scraps Backing - 24" x 46" (will not show) Batting - 24" x 46" (Tote) 1" x 120" (Handles) Lightweight Fusible Web - Scraps Small Bead - 1 (Bird's eye)		

20½

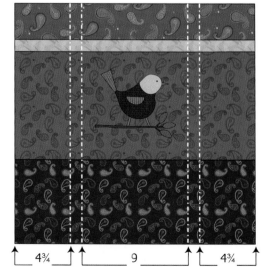

21½

4¾   9   4¾

Reduce your dependence on plastic and paper bags by using this stylish tote to bag your groceries and other purchases. Quilted layers and hefty straps make this tote as tough as it is attractive.

6. Sew three 4½" x 42" Fabric E strips together end-to-end to make one continuous 4½"-wide Fabric E strip. Press.

7. Fold handle strip in half lengthwise, press, and unfold. Bring raw edges to pressed line, press, fold again and press. Unfold piece, insert batting in center and refold strip. Topstitch ⅛" away from folded edge on both sides of handle. Determine the desired length of handle and cut two pieces to this measurement. Note: We cut our handles to 56" length.

8. Refer to diagram to the left to position and pin straps 4¾" from outside edge. Top stitch handles to tote stopping 1" from top edge. Handles will be reinforced after lining is sewn in place.

9. Place units from step 8 right sides together and stitch using ½"-wide seam along side and bottom edges leaving top edge free of stitches. Press seam open.

10. Fold one bottom corner of unit from step 1, matching side seam to bottom seam. Draw a 5" line across as shown. Sew on drawn line, anchoring stitches. Repeat for other corner.

11. Fold stitched corners to bottom seam of tote and tack in place for added stability.

Finishing the Tote

1. Using two 20½" x 21½" Fabric A Lining pieces, repeat Making the Tote steps 9 and 10 to make lining insert. Leave a 5" opening along side seam for turning.

2. Turn tote wrong side out. Position and pin lining inside tote, right sides together, making sure handles are free. Stitch lining and tote together along top edge using a ¼"-wide seam allowance. Turn right side out and press leaving ¼" of lining showing on front side of tote. Stitch along seam line of tote and lining to hold lining in place.

3. Referring to photo below to add reinforcing stitches to handles.

Day Brightener ... Lap Quilt

Fabric Requirements and Cutting Instructions

Read all instructions before beginning and use ¼"-wide seam allowances throughout. Read Cutting Strips and Pieces on page 92 prior to cutting fabric.

Getting Started

This quilt was designed to use one background fabric and eight different fat quarters in assorted colors but can be easily made using an assortment of background fabrics also. Refer to Accurate Seam Allowance on page 92. Whenever possible use Assembly Line Method on page 92. Press seams in direction of arrows.

A Friend Indeed Lap Quilt Finished Size: 56" x 66"	FIRST CUT		SECOND CUT	
	Number of Strips or Pieces	Dimensions	Number of Pieces	Dimensions
Fabric A Background 2⅛ yards or 8 Fat Quarters	12	6" x 42"	72	6" squares
Fabric B Unit Triangles Fat Quarter each of 8 Fabrics	3*	6" x 21" *cut for each fabric	9*	6" squares
Binding ⅝ yard	7	2¾" x 42"		
Backing - 3½ yards Batting - 62" x 72"				

Making the Quilt

1. Draw a diagonal line on wrong side of one 6" Fabric A square. Place marked square and one 6" Fabric B square right sides together. Sew scant ¼" away from drawn line on both sides to make half-square triangles as shown. Make seventy-two. Cut on drawn line and press. Square to 5½". This will make one hundred forty-four half-square triangle units, eighteen of each combination.

 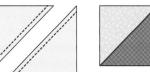

Fabric A = 6 x 6
Fabric B = 6 x 6
Make 72
(9 of each combination)

Square to 5½
Make 144
Half-square Triangles
(18 of each combinations)

2. Referring to photo, arrange units from step 1 in thirteen rows with eleven units each. Sew units into rows. Press seams in odd rows as shown and even rows in opposite direction.

Make 13 rows with assorted units.
Press odd rows as shown and even rows in opposite direction.

3. Referring to photo, sew rows together. Press.

Layering and Finishing

1. Cut backing crosswise into two equal pieces. Sew pieces together lengthwise to make one 63" x 80" (approximate) backing piece. Press.

2. Referring to Layering the Quilt on page 94, arrange and baste backing, batting, and top together. Hand or machine quilt as desired.

3. Refer to Binding the Quilt on page 94. Sew 2¾" x 42" binding strips end-to-end to make one continuous 2¾"-wide binding strip. Bind quilt to finish.

Colorful flags are flying on this flamboyant lap quilt. Eight fat quarters in a variety of colors are softened by a cream background. A single repeating block makes this quilt as fast as it is fun. Give the quilt to a friend or family member who needs a little special attention.

A FRIEND ••• INDEED Wall Quilt

A Friend Indeed Wall Quilt Finished Size: 39½" x 39½"	FIRST CUT		SECOND CUT	
	Number of Strips or Pieces	Dimensions	Number of Pieces	Dimensions
Fabric A Background ⅔ yard	2 4	4" x 42" 3½" x 42"	18 36	4" squares 3½" squares
Fabric B Friend Block ⅙ yard each of 3 Fabrics	1*	4" x 42" *cut for each fabric	4* 2* 4*	4" squares 3½" squares 1½" squares
Fabric C Friend Block ¼ yard	1 1	4" x 42" 1½" x 42"	6 3 4	4" squares 3½" squares 1½" squares
First Border ¼ yard	4	1¼" x 42"	2 2 4	1¼" x 39" 1¼" x 31½" 1¼" x 3½"
Outside Border & Sashing ¾ yard	4 6	3½" x 42" 1½" x 42"	4 4 24	3½" x 31½" 3½" squares 1½" x 9½"
Binding ½ yard	4	2¾" x 42"		
Backing - 1¼ yards (Fabric needs to be at least 44"-wide) or 2½" yards Pieced Batting - 44" x 44"				

Fabric Requirements and Cutting Instructions

Read all instructions before beginning and use ¼"-wide seam allowances throughout. Read Cutting Strips and Pieces on page 92 prior to cutting fabric.

Getting Started

When you need a quilt in a hurry to show your love and support to family or friends, this one fits the bill. It can be made in a variety of colors, a two-color combination, or make it as a group project. Block measures 9½" square (unfinished). Refer to Accurate Seam Allowance on page 92. Whenever possible use Assembly Line Method on page 92. Press seams in direction of arrows.

Making the Friend Block

1. Draw a diagonal line on wrong side of one 4" Fabric A square. Place marked square and one 4" Fabric B square right sides together. Sew scant ¼" away from drawn line on both sides to make half-square triangles as shown. Make four. Cut on drawn line and press. Square to 3½". This will make eight half-square triangle units.

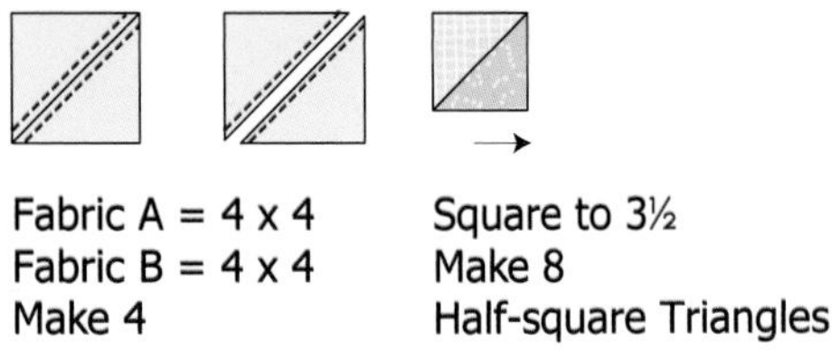
Fabric A = 4 x 4
Fabric B = 4 x 4
Make 4
Square to 3½
Make 8
Half-square Triangles

2. Sew one 3½" Fabric A square between two units from step 1 as shown. Press. Make four.

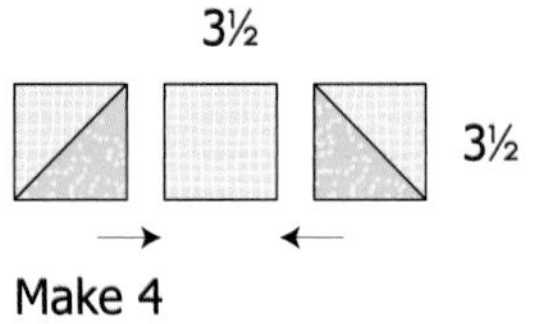
3½
3½
Make 4

3. Sew one 3½" Fabric B square between two 3½" Fabric A squares as shown. Press. Make two.

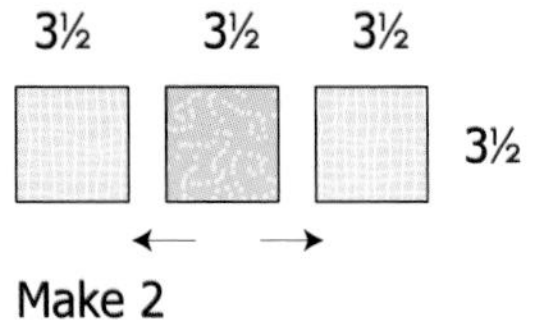
3½
3½
3½
3½
Make 2

Tell a friend that you care with this bright and happy wall quilt that is sure to bring smile after smile. Simple piecing in cheerful colors shows off hand or machine quilting beautifully. This is a great quilt for a group gift with each person making one block using the same background fabric but a different featured color.

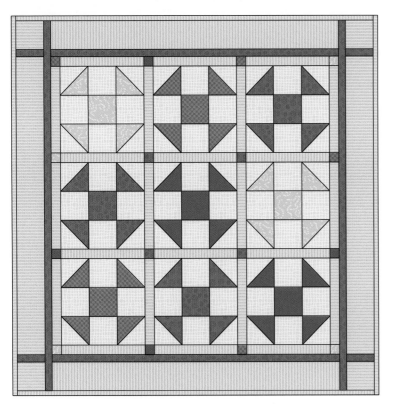

A Friend Indeed Wall Quilt
Finished Size: 39½" x 39½"

6. Draw a diagonal line on wrong side of one 4" Fabric A square. Place marked square and one 4" Fabric C square right sides together. Sew scant ¼" away from drawn line on both sides to make half-square triangles as shown. Make six. Cut on drawn line and press. Square to 3½". This will make twelve half-square triangle units.

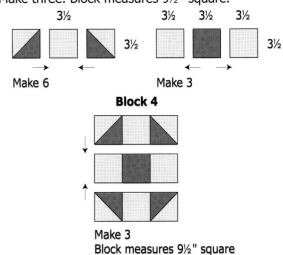

Fabric A = 4 x 4   Square to 3½
Fabric C = 4 x 4   Make 12
Make 6   Half-square Triangles

7. Sew one 3½" Fabric A square between two units from step 6 as shown. Press. Make six. Sew one 3½" Fabric C square between two 3½" Fabric A squares as shown. Press. Make three. Arrange and sew units together as shown. Press and label Block 4. Make three. Block measures 9½" square.

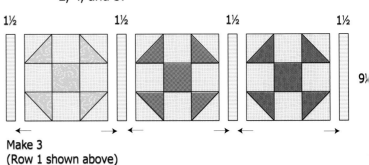

Make 6   Make 3

Block 4

Make 3
Block measures 9½" square

4. Sew one unit from step 3 between two units from step 2 as shown. Press and label Block 1. Make two. Block measures 9½" square.

Block 1

Make 2
Block measures 9½" square

Assembly

1. Referring to photo on page 61 and layout, arrange and sew together four 1½" x 9½" Sashing strips and three assorted Friend Blocks. Press. Make three. Block Row 1 uses Blocks 1, 2, and 4; Block Row 2 uses Blocks 4, 3, and 1; and Block Row 3 uses Blocks 2, 4, and 3.

1½   1½   1½   1½

Make 3
(Row 1 shown above)

5. Repeat steps 1-4 to make two of Block 2 and two of Block 3 as shown.

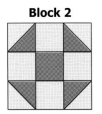

Block 2

Make 2
Block measures 9½" square

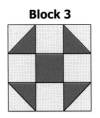

Block 3

Make 2
Block measures 9½" square

2. Referring to photo on page 61 and layout on page 62, arrange and sew together four 1½" assorted Fabric B and C squares and three 1½" x 9½" Sashing strips. Press. Make four Sashing rows.

| 1½ | 9½ | 1½ | 9½ | 1½ | 9½ | 1½ |

1½

Make 4

3. Referring to photo on page 61 and layout on page 62, arrange and sew together rows from steps 1 and 2. Press seams toward Sashing.

4. Sew one 1¼" x 31½" First Border strip to one 3½" x 31½" Outside Border strip. Press seams toward Outside Border. Make two. Referring to photo on page 61 and layout on page 62, sew units to top and bottom of quilt. Press.

5. Sew two 1¼" x 39" First Border strips to sides of quilt. Press seams toward border.

6. Referring to photo on page 61 and layout on page 62, arrange and sew together two 3½" Outside Border squares, two 1¼" x 3½" First Border strips, and one 3½" x 31½" Outside Border strip. Press seams toward Outside Border. Make two. Sew units to sides of quilt. Press.

Layering and Finishing

1. Referring to Layering the Quilt on page 94, arrange and baste backing, batting, and top together. Hand or machine quilt as desired.

2. Refer to Binding the Quilt on page 94. Use 2¾"-wide Binding strips to bind quilt.

> " A friend is one of the nicest things you can have, and one of the best things you can be. "
> Douglas Pagels

Quilters Care
• • • about friends

Life has its ups and downs. Show friends that you care...

♥ Buy a $2 primrose, wrap the pot in colored tissue paper and tie with a ribbon for a quick and pretty pick-me-up gift for a friend.

♥ Make her favorite cookies and deliver to her with a box of herbal tea. Stay and talk if she wants.

♥ Email a joke or a funny story to make her laugh.

♥ Bring homemade chicken soup to a friend who's feeling low.

♥ Share your chicken soup recipe with her when she's feeling better.

♥ Surprise a reader friend with a novel that you enjoyed.

♥ Arrange a spa day for the two of you for some much needed pampering.

♥ Distract her with a creative afternoon spent sewing, beading, scrapbooking, or some other craft.

♥ Give her a journal to record her thoughts and dreams.

♥ Frame a fun photo of her "support group" to be by her side all the time.

Birds of a Feather Lap Quilt Finished Size: 41" x 49"	FIRST CUT	
	Number of Strips or Pieces	Dimensions
Fabric A Green Strip ⅜ yard	3	3½" x 42"
Fabric B Pink Strip ¼ yard	1 2	3" x 42" 1½" x 42"
Fabric C Yellow Strip ¼ yard	3	1½" x 42"
Fabric D Purple Strip ½ yard	2 1	5½" x 42" 3½" x 42"
Fabric E Appliqué Cream Strip ½ yard	2	6½" x 42"
Fabric F Purple Strip ⅙ yard	2	2" x 42"
Fabric G Multi-Color Strip ¼ yard	1	4½" x 42"
Binding ½ yard	5	2¾" x 42"
Bird Appliqués - Assorted Scraps Backing - 2⅝ yards Batting - 47" x 55" Lightweight Fusible Web - ⅔ yard		

Fabric Requirements and Cutting Instructions

Read all instructions before beginning and use ¼"-wide seam allowances throughout. Read Cutting Strips and Pieces on page 92 prior to cutting fabric.

Getting Started

This quick and colorful quilt with its whimsical birds is fun to make and fun to give. Refer to Accurate Seam Allowance on page 92. Whenever possible use Assembly Line Method on page 92. Press seams in direction of arrows.

Making the Quilt

1. Refer to diagram below and photo to arrange strips in order shown. Sew together lengthwise three 3½" x 42" Fabric A strips, one 3" x 42" and two 1½" x 42" Fabric B strips, three 1½" x 42" Fabric C strips, two 5½" x 42" and one 3½" x 42" Fabric D strips, two 6½" x 42" Fabric E strips, two 2" x 42" Fabric F strips, and one 4½" x 42" Fabric G strip. Press.

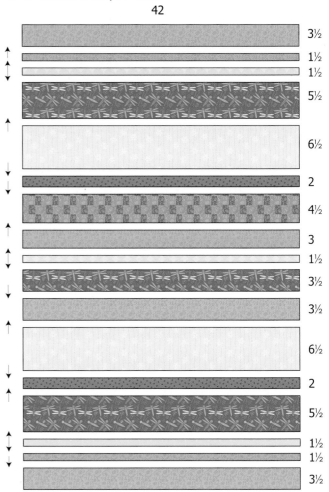

42

3½
1½
1½
5½
6½
2
4½
3
1½
3½
3½
6½
2
5½
1½
1½
3½

2. Trim quilt top to measure 40½" x 48½" making sure all selvages have been removed and corners are square.

3. Refer to appliqué instructions on page 93. Our instructions are for Quick-Fuse Appliqué, but if you prefer hand appliqué, reverse templates and add ¼"-wide seam allowances. Use birds' patterns on page 66 to trace four of Bird 1 and two reversed, and two of Bird 2 and two reversed on paper side of fusible web. Use appropriate fabrics to prepare all appliqués for fusing.

4. Refer to photo to position and fuse appliqués to quilt. Finish appliqué edges with machine satin stitch or other decorative stitching as desired.

Layering and Finishing

1. Cut backing crosswise into two equal pieces. Sew pieces together lengthwise to make one 47" x 80" (approximate) backing piece. Press and trim to 47" x 55".

2. Referring to Layering the Quilt on page 94, arrange and baste backing, batting, and top together. Hand or machine quilt as desired.

3. Refer to Binding the Quilt on page 94. Use 2¾"-wide Binding Strips to bind quilt.

Birds of a feather flock together and this cute quilt will give your friend a mood boost whenever she needs it. Whimsical birds line up to give messages of love and encouragement.

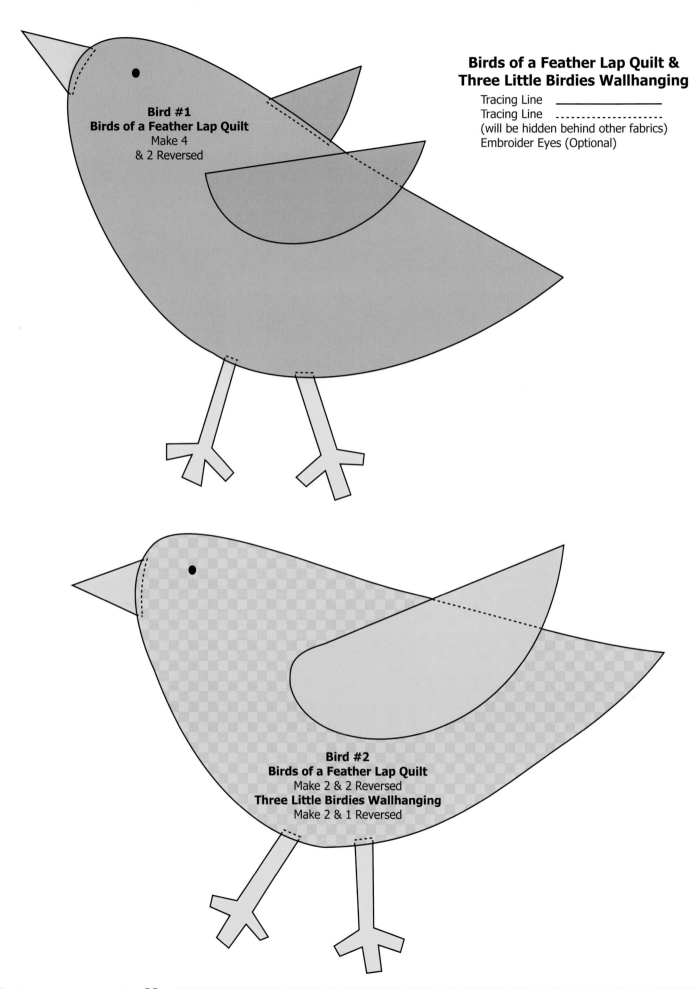

**Birds of a Feather Lap Quilt &
Three Little Birdies Wallhanging**

Tracing Line   —————————
Tracing Line   - - - - - - - - - - - - -
(will be hidden behind other fabrics)
Embroider Eyes (Optional)

Bird #1
Birds of a Feather Lap Quilt
Make 4
& 2 Reversed

Bird #2
Birds of a Feather Lap Quilt
Make 2 & 2 Reversed
Three Little Birdies Wallhanging
Make 2 & 1 Reversed

••• Wallhanging

Three Little Birdies Wallhanging Finished Size: 18" x 27"	FIRST CUT	
	Number of Strips or Pieces	Dimensions
Background ⅓ yard	1	7½" x 16½"
First Border ⅙ yard	2	1½" x 18½"
	2	1½" x 7½"
Outside Border ⅓ yard*	2*	4½" x 26½"
	2*	4½" x 9½"
Binding ⅓ yard	3	2¾" x 42"
Birdie Appliqués - Assorted Scraps Backing - ⅝ yard Batting - 22" x 31" Lightweight Fusible Web - ⅙ yard **If using a motif fabric adjust yardage and strip width to accommodate design elements, remembering to add ¼"-wide seam allowance to all sides.		

Three little birds sing songs of love, laughter, and friendship on this quick and quirky little quilt. Lively colors, perky patterns, and sweet songbirds provide lots of cheer with minimal sewing.

Getting Started

Three colorful little birdies play on a field of green in this delightful, quick-to-make, wallhanging. Read all instructions before beginning and use ¼"-wide seam allowances throughout.

Making the Wallhanging

Refer to appliqué instructions on page 93. Our instructions are for Quick-Fuse Appliqué, but if you prefer hand appliqué, reverse templates and add ¼"-wide seam allowances.

1. Sew 7½" x 16½" Background piece between two 1½" x 7½" First Border strips. Press seams toward border. Sew this unit between two 1½" x 18½" First Border strips. Press.

2. Sew unit from step 1 between two 4½" x 9½" Outside Border strips. Press toward border. Sew this unit between two 4½" x 26½" Outside Border strips. Press.

3. Use patterns on page 66 to trace two and one reversed of Bird #2 on paper side of fusible web. Use appropriate fabrics to prepare all appliqués for fusing.

4. Refer to photo to position and fuse appliqués to quilt. Finish appliqué edges with machine satin stitch or other decorative stitching as desired.

5. Referring to Layering the Quilt on page 94, arrange and baste backing, batting, and top together. Hand or machine quilt as desired.

6. Refer to Binding the Quilt on page 94. Use 2¾"-wide Binding strips to bind quilt.

Think Pink ... Lap Quilt

Think Pink Lap Quilt Finished Size: 47½" x 55¼"	FIRST CUT		SECOND CUT	
	Number of Strips or Pieces	Dimensions	Number of Pieces	Dimensions
■ Fabric A Block Centers ¼ yard	3	2¼" x 42"	45	2¼" squares
Fabric B Block Borders ⅓ yard each of 15 fabrics 	6*	1½" x 42" *cut for each fabric	6* 12* 12* 6*	1½" x 8¼" 1½" x 6¼" 1½" x 4¼" 1½" x 2¼"
■ Binding ⅝ yard	6	2¾" x 42"		
Backing - 3 yards Batting - 53" x 61"				

Fabric Requirements and Cutting Instructions

Read all instructions before beginning and use ¼"-wide seam allowances throughout. Read Cutting Strips and Pieces on page 92 prior to cutting fabric.

Getting Started

Show your support for those fighting cancer by making this easy-to-construct quilt. Block measures 8¼" square (unfinished). Refer to Accurate Seam Allowance on page 92. Whenever possible use Assembly Line Method on page 92. Press seams in direction of arrows.

Making the Blocks

Each block uses the same fabric for the center and three different Fabric B strips for block borders. Only forty-two blocks are used in the quilt.

1. Sew one 2¼" Fabric A square between two matching 1½" x 2¼" Fabric B pieces as shown. Press. Make forty-five in assorted combinations.

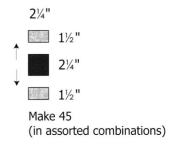

2¼"
1½"
2¼"
1½"

Make 45
(in assorted combinations)

2. Sew one unit from step 1 between two matching 1½" x 4¼" Fabric B pieces as shown. Press. Make forty-five in assorted combinations.

1½"   1½"

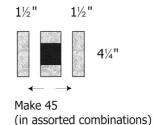

4¼"

Make 45
(in assorted combinations)

3. Sew one unit from step 2 between two 1½" x 4¼" Fabric B pieces as shown. Fabric B strips are different than those in step 2 but match each other. Press. Make forty-five in assorted combinations.

4¼"

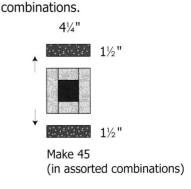

1½"

1½"

Make 45
(in assorted combinations)

Pink ribbons have long been associated with breast cancer research and awareness and this quilt takes "pink" to a whole new level. Funky feminine prints and a steadfast geometric design combine to portray the strength, tenacity, and beauty of women affected by breast cancer.

4. Sew one unit from step 3 between two matching 1½" x 6¼" Fabric B pieces as shown. Press. Make forty-five in assorted combinations.

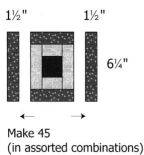

Make 45
(in assorted combinations)

5. Sew one unit from step 4 between two 1½" x 6¼" Fabric B pieces as shown. Fabric B strips are different then those in step 4 but match each other. Press. Make forty-five in assorted combinations.

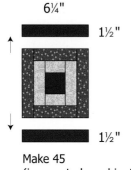

Make 45
(in assorted combinations)

6. Sew one unit from step 5 between two matching 1½" x 8¼" Fabric B strips as shown. Press. Make forty-five in assorted combinations. Block measure 8¼" square. Forty-two blocks will be used for this project.

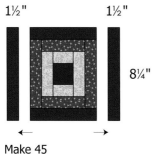

Make 45
(in assorted combinations)

Assembling the Quilt

Extra blocks are made to give fabric placement options when laying out the quilt. Before sewing, lay out the blocks on a design wall to determine the best overall arrangement for the quilt. Use extra blocks for a small project or use them in a scrappy quilt.

1. Refer to photo on page 69 to arrange blocks in seven rows with six blocks each. Note: Blocks are turned 90-degrees from block to block and row-to-row so block border seams don't line up.

2. Sew blocks into rows. Press seams in opposite directions from row to row.

3. Sew rows together and press.

Layering and Finishing

1. Cut backing crosswise into two equal pieces. Sew pieces together lengthwise to make one 54" x 80" (approximate) backing piece. Press and trim to 54" x 61".

2. Referring to Layering the Quilt on page 94, arrange and baste backing, batting, and top together. Hand or machine quilt as desired.

3. Refer to Binding the Quilt on page 94. Sew 2¾" x 42" binding strips end-to-end to make one continuous 2¾"-wide binding strip. Bind quilt to finish.

" The power of love to change bodies is legendary, built into folklore, common sense, and everyday experience. Love moves the flesh, it pushes matter around...Throughout history, "tender loving care" has uniformly been recognized as a valuable element in healing."

Larry Dossey

Pink Wishes
... Wall Quilt

One piece at a time, wishes for health, hope, and happiness make up these pink flowers. Left-over strips from the Think Pink Quilt were used to create this fun and flirty little quilt that will be a mood-booster for any woman.

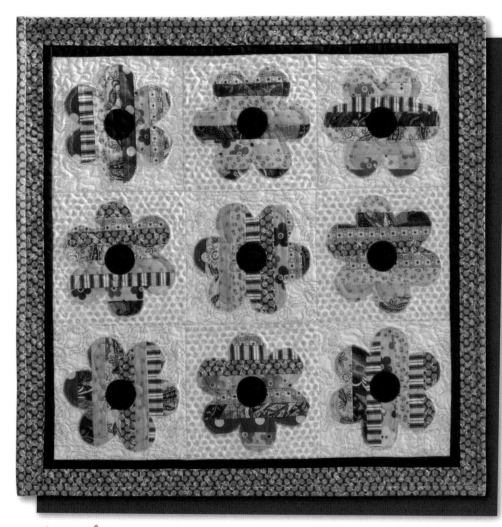

Pink Wishes Wall Quilt
Finished Size: 25" x 25"

Fabric Requirements and Cutting Instructions

Read all instructions before beginning and use ¼"-wide seam allowances throughout. Read Cutting Strips and Pieces on page 92 prior to cutting fabric. Cutting chart is on page 72.

Getting Started

This quilt is quick, easy, and fun to make. Refer to Accurate Seam Allowance on page 92. Whenever possible use Assembly Line Method on page 92. Press seams in direction of arrows.

Making the Quilt

1. Sew one 7½" Fabric B square between two 7½" Fabric A squares as shown. Press. Make two.

7½   7½   7½

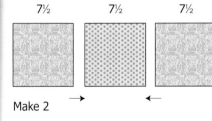

7½

Make 2   →   ←

2. Sew one 7½" Fabric A square between two 7½" Fabric B squares as shown. Press.

7½   7½   7½

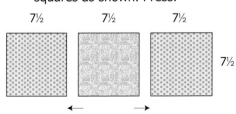

7½

←   →

3. Referring to photo, sew unit from step 2 between two units from step 1. Press.

Pink Wishes Wall Quilt Finished Size: 22" x 22"	FIRST CUT		SECOND CUT	
	Number of Strips or Pieces	Dimensions	Number of Pieces	Dimensions
Fabric A Background ¼ yard	1	7½" x 42"	5	7½" squares
Fabric B Background ¼ yard	1	7½" x 42"	4	7½" squares
Flower Appliqué ⅛ yard or Assorted Scraps (fifteen fabrics)	3*	1¼" x 12½" *cut for each fabric Note: Leftover strips from Pink Ribbon quilt can be cut for Flower Appliqué strips		
Accent Border ⅙ yard	4	1" x 42"		
Outside Border ¼ yard	4	1½" x 42"		
Binding ⅜ yard	4	2¾" x 42"		

Flower Center Appliqués - Assorted Scraps
Backing - ⅞ yard
Batting - 29" x 29"
Lightweight Fusible Web or Mistyfuse™ - 1 yard

Adding the Appliqués

Refer to appliqué instructions on page 93 and Mistyfuse™ on page 94. Our instructions are for Quick-Fuse Appliqué, but if you prefer hand appliqué add ¼"-wide seam allowances.

1. Sew lengthwise forty-five 1¼" x 12½" assorted fabric strips to make a piece that measures approximately 33" x 12½". Use patterns on page 73 to trace nine flowers and nine flower centers on paper side of fusible web or freezer paper. Use strip unit for flowers and desired fabric for centers to prepare all appliqués for fusing.

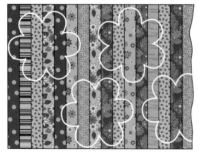

2. Refer to photo on page 71 to position and fuse appliqués to quilt. Finish appliqué edges with machine satin stitch or other decorative stitching as desired.

Adding the Borders

1. Refer to Adding the Borders on page 94. Measure quilt through center from side to side. Cut two 1" x 42" First Border strips to this measurement. Sew to top and bottom of quilt. Press seams toward border.

Women are working hard to raise awareness of breast cancer and to fund research to find a cure. One of the many ways that women are supporting this cause is through quilts. From cruises and events to quilt auctions and raffles, quilters are finding many ways to use their craft to help fund a cure and to bring comfort to those affected.

For instance, quilt makers in Northern California have raised hundreds of thousands of dollars for breast cancer research and patient treatment programs through quilt auctions held every three years. Many of the quilts are made to honor a loved one lost to cancer or in celebration of the quilter's personal successes in overcoming this disease.

Other quilters are providing comfort and support to breast cancer patients by donating quilts to provide emotional and physical warmth during breast cancer treatments.

Opportunities to help the breast cancer cause through quilting and volunteering abound. Check with local quilt guilds, cancer research and treatment centers, a Susan G. Komen Race for a Cure affiliate, or your local American Cancer Society office to find out about programs near you.

2. Measure quilt through center from top to bottom including border just added. Cut two 1"-wide First Border strips to this measurement. Sew to sides of quilt. Press.

3. Refer to steps 1 and 2 to measure, trim, and sew 1½"-wide Outside Border strips to top, bottom, and sides of quilt. Press.

Layering and Finishing

1. Referring to Layering the Quilt on page 94, arrange and baste backing, batting, and top together. Hand or machine quilt as desired.

2. Refer to Binding the Quilt on page 94. Use 2¾"-wide Binding strips to bind quilt.

**Pink Wishes
Wall Quilt**

Tracing Line _____

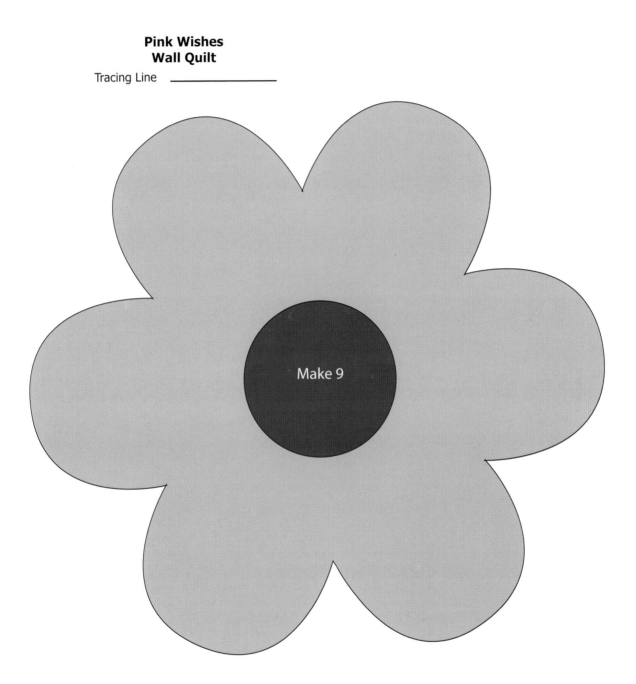

Make 9

Stars of Honor ··· Lap Quilt

Stars of Honor Lap Quilt Finished Size: 54½" x 70½"	FIRST CUT		SECOND CUT	
	Number of Strips or Pieces	Dimensions	Number of Pieces	Dimensions
Fabric A Background 2⅛ yards	5 6	8½" x 42" 4½" x 42"	18 24 4	8½" squares 4½" x 8½" 4½" squares
Fabric B Star Points 1½ yards	11	4½" x 42"	88	4½" squares
Fabric C Star Center Background ⅞ yard	11	2½" x 42"	20 116	2½" x 4½" 2½" squares
Fabric D Star Center Red ¾ yard	9	2½" x 42"	52 32	2½" x 4½" 2½" squares
Fabric E Star Center Tan ⅝ yard	8	2½" x 42"	16 84	2½" x 4½" 2½" squares
Fabric F Star Center Brown ½ yard	6	2½" x 42"	16 60	2½" x 4½" 2½" squares
First Border ⅓ yard	6	1¼" x 42"		
Outside Border ⅝ yard	7	2½" x 42"		
Binding ⅝ yard	7	2¾" x 42"		
Backing - 3½ yards Batting - 62" x 78"				

Fabric Requirements and Cutting Instructions

Read all instructions before beginning and use ¼"-wide seam allowances throughout. Read Cutting Strips and Pieces on page 92 prior to cutting fabric.

Getting Started

This quilt features Liberty, Freedom, Glory, and Honor Blocks showcased in the center of each large star and is a must-have quilt for any military family. Star Center Blocks measure 8½" square (unfinished). Large Star Blocks measure 8½" square and 4½" x 8½" (unfinished). Refer to Accurate Seam Allowance on page 92. Whenever possible use Assembly Line Method on page 92. Press seams in direction of arrows.

Making the Star Center Blocks
Liberty Block

1. Refer to Quick Corner Triangles on page 92. Making quick corner triangle units, sew one 2½" Fabric E square and one 2½" Fabric F square to one 2½" x 4½" Fabric C piece as shown. Press. Make twenty.

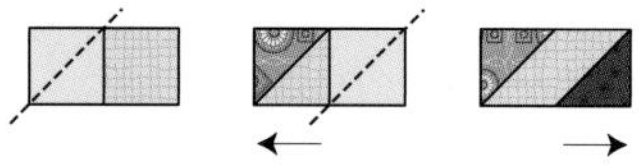

Fabric E = 2½ x 2½
Fabric F = 2½ x 2½
Fabric C = 2½ x 4½
Make 20

2. Making a quick corner triangle unit, sew one 2½" Fabric C square to one 2½" x 4½" Fabric D piece as shown. Press. Make twenty.

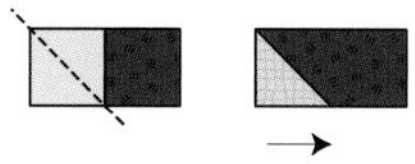

Fabric C = 2½ x 2½
Fabric D = 2½ x 4½
Make 20

3. Sew one unit from step 1 to one unit from step 2 as shown. Press. Make twenty. Sew two of these units together as shown. Press. Make ten.

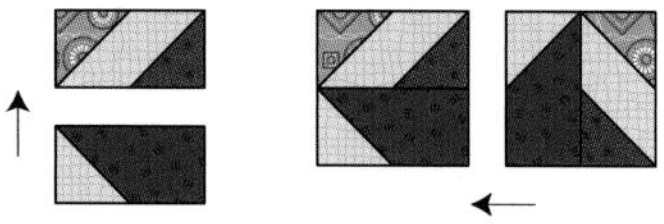

Make 20   Make 10

4. Sew two units from step 3 together as shown. Refer to Twisting Seams on page 92. Press. Make five. Liberty Block measures 8½" square.

Liberty Block

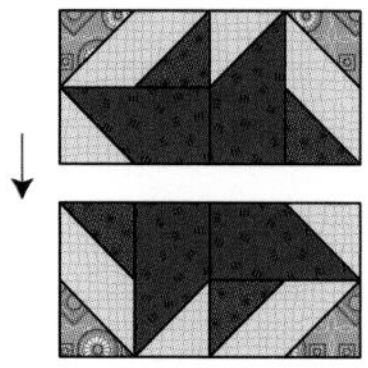

Make 5
Block measures 8½"

Welcome them home and thank them for their service by making red, white, and blue quilts for members of the armed services. Four different blocks are set into stars of blue on this handsome and meaningful quilt. If you prefer, use only one block for star centers or repeat just one block for a completely different quilt like the Veteran's Quilt on page 81.

Freedom Block

1. Making quick corner triangle units, sew two 2½" Fabric D squares to one 2½" x 4½" Fabric E piece as shown. Press. Make sixteen.

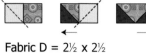

Fabric D = 2½ x 2½
Fabric E = 2½ x 4½
Make 16

2. Sew one unit from step 1 between two 2½" Fabric E squares as shown. Press. Make eight.

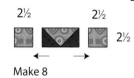

2½   2½

2½

Make 8

3. Making a quick corner triangle unit, sew one 2½" Fabric C square to one 2½" Fabric F square as shown. Press. Make eight.

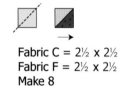

Fabric C = 2½ x 2½
Fabric F = 2½ x 2½
Make 8

4. Sew one unit from step 3 to one 2½" Fabric C square as shown. Press. Make eight. Sew two of these units together as shown. Press. Make four.

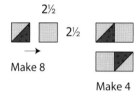

2½

2½

Make 8

Make 4

5. Sew one unit from step 4 between two units from step 1 as shown. Press. Make four.

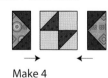

Make 4

6. Sew one unit from step 5 between two units from step 2 as shown. Press. Make four. Freedom Block measures 8½" square.

Freedom Block

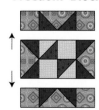

Make 4
Block measures 8½" square

Glory Block

1. Making quick corner triangle units, sew two 2½" Fabric C squares to one 2½" x 4½" Fabric F piece as shown. Press. Make sixteen.

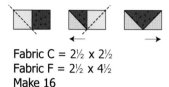

Fabric C = 2½ x 2½
Fabric F = 2½ x 4½
Make 16

2. Making quick corner triangle units, sew one 2½" Fabric E square and one 2½" Fabric C square to one 2½" x 4½" Fabric D piece as shown. Press. Make sixteen.

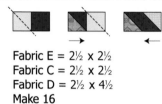

Fabric E = 2½ x 2½
Fabric C = 2½ x 2½
Fabric D = 2½ x 4½
Make 16

3. Sew one unit from step 1 to one unit from step 2 together as shown. Press. Make sixteen. Sew two of these units together as shown. Press. Make eight.

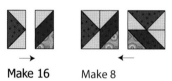

Make 16   Make 8

4. Sew two units from step 3 together as shown. Press. Make four. Glory Block measures 8½" square.

Glory Block

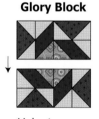

Make 4
Block measures 8½" square

Honor Block

1. Making a quick corner triangle unit, sew one 2½" Fabric E square to one 2½" Fabric F square as shown. Press. Make sixteen.

Fabric E = 2½ x 2½
Fabric F = 2½ x 2½
Make 16

2. Making a quick corner triangle unit, sew one 2½" Fabric C square to one 2½" Fabric F square as shown. Press. Make sixteen.

Fabric C = 2½ x 2½
Fabric F = 2½ x 2½
Make 16

3. Sew one unit from step 1 to one unit from step 2 as shown. Press. Make sixteen.

Make 16

4. Making quick corner triangle units, sew one 2½" Fabric E square and one 2½" Fabric C square to one 2½" x 4½" Fabric D piece as shown. Press. Make sixteen.

Fabric E = 2½ x 2½
Fabric C = 2½ x 2½
Fabric D = 2½ x 4½
Make 16

Stars of Honor Lap Quilt
Finished Size: 54½" x 70½"

5. Sew one unit from step 3 to one unit from step 4 as shown. Press. Make sixteen. Sew two of these units together as shown. Press. Make eight.

Make 16   Make 8

6. Sew two units from step 4 together as shown. Twist Seams. Press. Make four. Honor Block measures 8½" square.

Honor Block

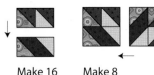

Make 4

Making the Star Blocks

1. Refer to Quick Corner Triangles on page 92. Making quick corner triangle units, sew three 4½" Fabric B squares to one 8½" Fabric A square as shown. Press. Make four. Star Block 1 measures 8½" square.

Star Block 1

Fabric B = 4½ x 4½
Fabric A = 8½ x 8½
Make 4
Block measures 8½" square

2. Making quick corner triangle units, sew four 4½" Fabric B squares to one 8½" Fabric A square as shown. Press. Make fourteen. Star Block 2 measures 8½" square.

Star Block 2

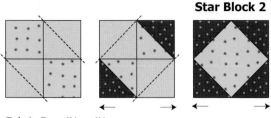

Fabric B = 4½ x 4½
Fabric A = 8½ x 8½
Make 14
Block measures 8½" square

3. Making quick corner triangle units, sew two 4½" Fabric B squares to one 4½" x 8½" Fabric A piece as shown. Press. Make ten. Star Block 3 measures 4½" x 8½".

Star Block 3

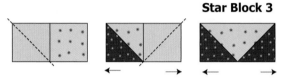

Fabric B = 4½ x 4½
Fabric A = 4½ x 8½
Make 10
Block measures 8½" square

Assembling the Quilt

It is recommended to layout the entire quilt prior to sewing rows together. Refer to photo on page 75 and layout on page 77 to arrange Fabric A pieces, Star Blocks, and star center blocks (Liberty, Freedom, Glory, and Honor Blocks) as desired.

"Let us solemnly remember the sacrifices of all those who fought so valiantly, on the seas, in the air, and on foreign shores, to preserve our heritage of freedom, and let us reconsecrate ourselves to the task of promoting an enduring peace so that their efforts shall not have been in vain."

Dwight D Eisenhower

1. Arrange and sew together two 4½" Fabric A squares, three 4½" x 8½" Fabric A pieces, and two of Star Block 3 as shown. Press. Make two and label Rows 1 and 9.

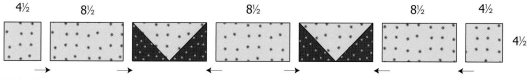

Make 2
Rows 1 & 9

2. Arrange and sew together two 4½" x 8½" Fabric A pieces, two of Star Block 1, two assorted star center blocks, and one Star Block 2 as shown. Press. Make two and label Rows 2 and 8. One row will be rotated 180° when sewing quilt together.

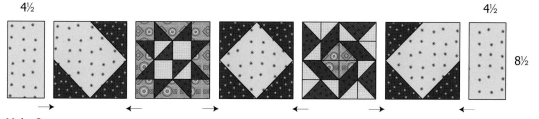

Make 2
Rows 2 & 8 (using assorted star center blocks)

3. Arrange and sew together two of Star Block 3, three assorted star center blocks, and two of Star Block 2 as shown. Press. Make three and label Rows 3, 5, and 7.

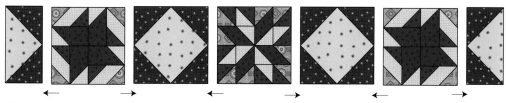

Make 3
Rows 3, 5 & 7 (using assorted star center blocks)

4. Arrange and sew together two 4½" X 8½" Fabric A pieces, three of Star Block 2, and two assorted star center blocks as shown. Press. Make two and label Rows 4 and 6.

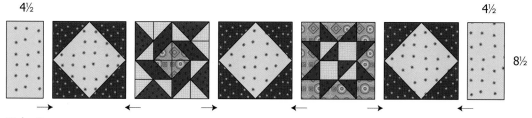

Make 2
Rows 4 & 6 (using assorted star center blocks)

5. Referring to photo on page 75 and layout on page 77, sew rows together. Press.

Adding the Borders

1. Refer to Adding the Borders on page 94. Sew 1¼" x 42" First Border strips together end-to-end to make one continuous 1¼"-wide First Border strip. Measure quilt through center from side to side. Cut two 1¼"-wide First Border strips to this measurement. Sew to top and bottom of quilt. Press seams toward border.

2. Measure quilt through center from top to bottom including border just added. Cut two 1¼"-wide First Border strips to this measurement. Sew to sides of quilt. Press.

3. Refer to steps 1 and 2 to join, measure, trim, and sew 2½"-wide Outside Border strips to top, bottom, and sides of quilt. Press.

Layering and Finishing

1. Cut backing crosswise into two equal pieces. Sew pieces together lengthwise to make one 63" x 80" (approximate) backing piece.

2. Referring to Layering the Quilt on page 94, arrange and baste backing, batting, and top together. Hand or machine quilt as desired.

3. Refer to Binding the Quilt on page 94. Sew 2¾" x 42" binding strips end-to-end to make one continuous 2¾"-wide binding strip. Bind quilt to finish.

Quilters Care
• • • by Labeling their Quilts

Attaching a label to your donation quilt will give you the opportunity to send a message of encouragement to the recipient as well as serve to personalize the quilt. From the label the recipient will know who pieced the quilt, when and where it was made, who quilted the quilt and any other information that you may want to include. A label also serves as historical documentation for the quilt letting future generations know who made it and why it was made.

★ ★ Made with Love ★ ★

Permanent Marking Pens
You can write directly onto your cloth label with a permanent marker like Pigma Micron Pens. Place cloth label on a piece of sandpaper to hold it in place while writing.

Embroidery
Hand or machine embroider your label.

Computer Generated Labels
In this transfer print procedure the label is designed on your computer and printed directly onto special fabric sheets using an inkjet printer. There are several different manufacturers that offer 100% cotton, silk, and poplin fabric sheets. Pay close attention to the finishing process to set the color, if not set properly the color can wash out.

Copier Label
To use label above, ask your local copier shop to print a mirror image copy of the label onto photo transfer paper. Follow directions on the paper to transfer the image to your fabric. Write information onto label using a pigma pen.

Hand appliqué label to the back of quilt. Many quilters affix the label before quilting so that it becomes a permanent part of the quilt.

Permission is granted by Debbie Mumm Inc. to copy page 80 to successfully complete this project.

Veteran's ··· Lap Quilt

Honor those that served - make lap quilts for military veterans who are in a veteran's home or hospital or right next door. Warm, masculine, and interesting, this quilt will be appreciated and enjoyed by those that served our nation well.

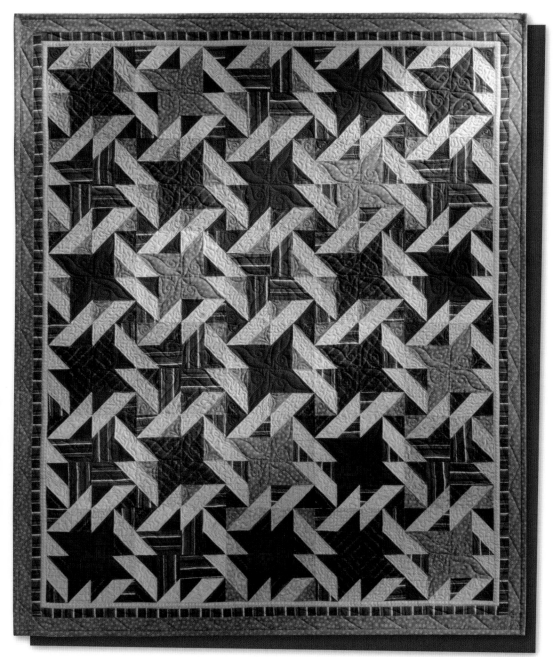

Veteran's Lap Quilt
Finished Size: 46" x 54"

Fabric Requirements and Cutting Instructions

Read all instructions before beginning and use ¼"-wide seam allowances throughout. Read Cutting Strips and Pieces on page 92 prior to cutting fabric. Cutting chart is on page 82.

Getting Started

Scrappy Stars abound in this quilt featuring the Liberty Block; one of the virtues Veterans hold dear. Block measures 8½" square (unfinished). Refer to Accurate Seam Allowance on page 92. Whenever possible use Assembly Line Method on page 92. Press seams in direction of arrows.

Making the Liberty Block

This scrappy quilt block construction is made up of two different units. Fabrics within each block match to create a uniform block. Extra Fabric A squares and pieces, and 2½" x 4½" Fabric B pieces were cut to allow for the play of fabrics within the blocks. Mix and match fabrics as desired.

Veteran's Lap Quilt Finished Size: 46" x 54"	FIRST CUT		SECOND CUT	
	Number of Strips or Pieces	Dimensions	Number of Pieces	Dimensions
Fabric A Background ½ yard each of 4 fabrics	6*	2½" x 42" *cut for each fabric	32* 32*	2½" x 4½" 2½" squares
Fabric B Stars ⅔ yard each of 4 fabrics	8*	2½" x 42" *cut for each fabric	32* 64*	2½" x 4½" 2½" squares
First Border ¼ yard	5	1" x 42"		
Second Border ¼ yard	5	1¼" x 42"		
Outside Border ⅓ yard	5	1¾" x 42"		
Binding ⅝ yard	6	2¾" x 42"		
Backing - 3 yards Batting - 52" x 60"				

1. Refer to Quick Corner Triangles on page 92. Making quick corner triangle units, sew one 2½" Fabric B square and one different 2½" Fabric B square to one 2½" x 4½" Fabric A piece as shown. Press. Make four, matching Unit 1 fabrics.

Unit 1

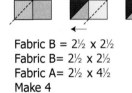

Fabric B = 2½ x 2½
Fabric B= 2½ x 2½
Fabric A= 2½ x 4½
Make 4
(matching units)

2. Making a quick corner triangle unit, sew one 2½" Fabric A square to one 2½" x 4½" Fabric B piece as shown. Press. Make four, matching Unit 2 fabrics.

Unit 2

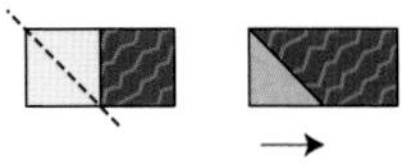

Fabric A = 2½ x 2½
Fabric B= 2½ x 4½
Make 4
(matching units)

3. Sew one Unit 1 to one Unit 2 as shown. Press. Make four. Sew two of these units together as shown. Press. Make two.

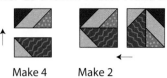

Make 4   Make 2

4. Sew two units from step 3 together as shown. Press. Refer to Twisting Seams on page 92. Make a total of thirty-two blocks using assorted fabric combinations and matching fabric in units within each block. Only thirty blocks will be used in the quilt. Block measures 8½" square.

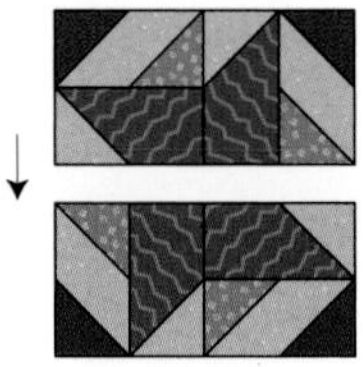

Make 32
(Only 30 will be used in this project. Use assorted fabric combinations to make block.)
Block measures 8½"

5. Refer to photo on page 81 and layout on page 83 to arrange blocks in six rows with five blocks each. Sew blocks together into rows. Press seams in opposite direction from row to row.

6. Referring to photo on page 81 and layout on page 83, sew rows together. Press.

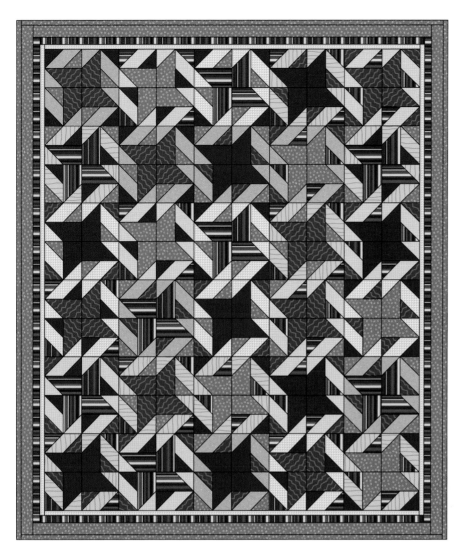

Veteran's Lap Quilt
Finished Size: 46" x 54"

Adding the Borders

1. Refer to Adding the Borders on page 94. Sew 1" x 42" First Border strips together end-to-end to make one continuous 1"-wide First Border strip. Measure quilt through center from side to side. Cut two 1"-wide First Border strips to this measurement. Sew to top and bottom of quilt. Press seams toward border.

2. Measure quilt through center from top to bottom including border just added. Cut two 1"-wide First Border strips to this measurement. Sew to sides of quilt. Press.

3. Refer to steps 1 and 2 to join, measure, trim, and sew 1¼"-wide Second Border strips, and 1¾"-wide Outside Border strips to top, bottom, and sides of quilt. Press.

Layering and Finishing

1. Cut backing crosswise into two equal pieces. Sew pieces together lengthwise to make one 54" x 80" (approximate) backing piece. Press and trim to 54" x 60".

2. Referring to Layering the Quilt on page 94, arrange and baste backing, batting, and top together. Hand or machine quilt as desired.

3. Refer to Binding the Quilt on page 94. Sew 2¾" x 42" binding strips end-to-end to make one continuous 2¾"-wide binding strip. Bind quilt to finish.

> "Let no one be discouraged by the belief that there is nothing one man or one woman can do against the enormous array of the world's ills...Few will have the greatness to bend history itself; but each of us can work to change a small portion of events, and in the total of all those acts will be written the history of this generation..."
>
> Robert F Kennedy

Staying Centered ... Lap Quilt

Staying Centered Circle Lap Quilt Finished Size: 39" x 51"	FIRST CUT	
	Number of Strips or Pieces	Dimensions
Background Fat Quarter each of 18 fabrics	6*	3½" x 6½" *cut for each fabric
Border ⅓ yard	3	1½" x 42"
	2	1½" x 36½"
Binding ½ yard	5	2¾" x 42"
Circle Appliqués - Assorted scraps Backing - 2½ yards Batting - 45" x 57" Lightweight Fusible Web or Mistyfuse™ - 1 yard		

Fabric Requirements and Cutting Instructions

Read all instructions before beginning and use ¼"-wide seam allowances throughout. Read Cutting Strips and Pieces on page 92 prior to cutting fabric.

Getting Started

Life is an interplay of good times and bad and trying to stay centered and focused with every change that occurs. This quilt depicts this with its multi-colored woven design using fabrics in various shades of darks to light - an interesting backdrop for the circle appliqués. Block measures 6½" square (unfinished). Refer to Accurate Seam Allowance on page 92. Whenever possible use Assembly Line Method on page 92. Press seams in direction of arrows.

"Love yourself first and everything else falls into line."
Lucille Ball

Making the Quilt

Extra blocks are made to give fabric placement options when laying out the quilt. Before sewing, lay out the blocks on a design wall to determine the best overall arrangement of the blocks and circles. Use extra blocks for a small project or use them in a scrappy quilt.

1. Sew two different 3½" x 6½" Background pieces together as shown. Press. Make six matching pairs. Repeat step to make a total of fifty-four blocks, six each of nine different pairs of background fabrics. This quilt uses forty-eight blocks.

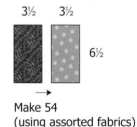

Make 54
(using assorted fabrics)

Make 6 Make 6 Make 6

Make 6 Make 6 Make 6

Make 6 Make 6 Make 6
(48 will be used for this quilt)

2. Refer to photo and layout on page 86 to arrange and sew together eight rows with six blocks each. Press seams in opposite direction from row to row.

3. Sew rows from step 2 together. Press.

Taking care of ourselves is one of the best things we can do for those who depend on us. This quilt with its earthy color scheme, simple balanced background, and circular appliqués will remind us to stay centered, grounded, and strong. Have fun picking out 18 fat quarters for this delightful quilt.

Adding the Appliqués

Refer to appliqué instructions on page 93 and Mistyfuse™ on page 94. Our instructions are for Quick-Fuse Appliqué, but if you prefer hand appliqué, add ¼"-wide seam allowances.

1. Use patterns on page 95 to trace four 5½", seven 4½", five 3½", six 2½", and three 2" circles on paper side of fusible web or freezer paper. Use appropriate fabrics to prepare all appliqués for fusing.

2. Refer to photo on page 85 and layout to position and fuse appliqués to quilt. Finish appliqué edges with machine satin stitch or other decorative stitching as desired.

Adding the Borders

1. Refer to Adding the Borders on page 94. Sew 1½" x 36½" Border strips to top and bottom of quilt. Press seams toward border.

2. Sew 1½" x 42" Border strips together end-to-end to make one continuous 1½"-wide Border strip. Press. Measure quilt through center from top to bottom including border just added. Cut two 1½"-wide Border strips to this measurement. Sew to top and bottom of quilt. Press.

Layering and Finishing

1. Cut backing crosswise into two equal pieces. Sew pieces together lengthwise to make one 45" x 80" (approximate) backing piece. Press and trim to 45" x 57".

2. Referring to Layering the Quilt on page 94, arrange and baste backing, batting, and top together. Hand or machine quilt as desired.

3. Refer to Binding the Quilt on page 94. Sew 2¾" x 42" binding strips end-to-end to make one continuous 2¾"-wide binding strip. Bind quilt to finish.

Staying Centered
Lap Quilt
Finished Size: 39" x 51"

" Our lives are not determined by what happens to us but by how we react to what happens, not by what life brings to us, but by the attitude we bring to life. A positive attitude causes a chain reaction of positive thoughts, events, and outcomes. It is a catalyst, a spark that creates extraordinary results. "

Martin Buber

Quilters Care

Women tend to be the caretakers of the home and the caregivers for children, the sick, and the elderly...no wonder we sometimes become careworn! Taking care of ourselves is one of the best things we can do for those who depend on us. Staying centered is all about self-care so that we can mentally and physically stay on track. These strategies will help you fit self-care into your days to energize you against the emotional and physical tolls of stress and exhaustion.

♥ **Exercise Regularly.**
Exercise not only keeps you fit, but researchers found that it also releases endorphins that keep you happy. Schedule mini-workouts throughout the day, take a walk, work out to a tape or DVD, or go to the gym.

♥ **Try Something New.**
Challenge yourself by taking a class, trying a new sport, or learning a new skill.

♥ **Make Time for Hobbies.**
"Down time" is important and hobbies like quilting are a great distraction.

♥ **Nurture Friends.**
Friends can pick you up when you are down, offer valuable insights, make you laugh, and add lots of fun to your life.

♥ **Adjust your Attitude.**
When you feel yourself getting stressed and tense, breathe deeply, release the tension in your body and consciously adjust your attitude to be positive and upbeat.

♥ **Seek out Enriching Sensory Experiences.**
Music, fragrance, texture, and taste, a spa treatment, a symphony performance, a romp with the dog will all help you live in and appreciate the moment.

♥ **Count your Blessings.**
Many people find keeping a journal to be a soul-satisfying way to release feelings, think through problems, and count their blessings.

Staying Centered ··· Laptop Tote

A laptop can be a lifeline for friends and family when someone has a challenge in life. With this stylish and functional tote, it's easy to carry a laptop with you.

Staying Centered Laptop Tote Finished Size: 15" x 12" x 2½"	FIRST CUT	
	Number of Strips or Pieces	Dimensions
Background ½ yard	1	16½" x 36½"
Lining ½ yard	1	16½" x 36½"
Strap ½ yard	4	3½" x 42"
Flower Appliqués - Assorted Scraps Fusible Ultra Firm Stabilizer - 1⅛ yards Batting - 18" x 38" 3½" x 64" Lightweight Fusible Web - ½ yard Bag Closure		

Fabric Requirements and Cutting Instructions

Read all instructions before beginning and use ¼"-wide seam allowances throughout. Read Cutting Strips and Pieces on page 92 prior to cutting fabric.

Getting Started

Carry your laptop in style with this attractive tote. The tote is reversible and features a wide shoulder strap for weight distribution. Tote size can be adjusted to fit your laptop; ours fits up to a 17" laptop (diagonal measurement). A walking foot is recommended for quilting and adding the straps. Refer to Accurate Seam Allowance on page 92.

Making the Tote

There are many ultra firm stabilizers on the market. For this project we used Pellon Peltex 70. This product is firm, smooth, easy to cut, and machine washable. It's great for crafts, bags, and dimensional items like bowls. All edges are finished before the body of the bag and strap are sewn together. No corners were clipped when adding the strap to the laptop bag during construction.

1. Refer to circle templates on page 95 to trace one 3½" circle on template plastic or pattern paper.

2. Place 3½" circle on one corner (side 'D') of 16½" x 36½" Background fabric piece as shown. Trace circle's outside curve and cut to make a rounded corner. Repeat for adjoining corner. Only one end of the bag will have curved edges. This curved end will become the bag flap.

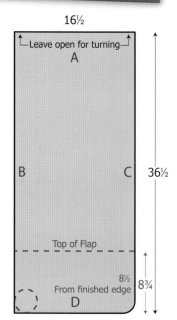

16½

Leave open for turning

A

B   C   36½

Top of Flap

8½

8¾

From finished edge

D

3. Refer to appliqué instructions on page 93. Our instructions are for Quick-Fuse Appliqué, but if you prefer hand appliqué, add ¼"-wide seam allowances. Use patterns on pages 90 and 91 to trace one of each flower and one of each leaf on paper side of fusible web. Use appropriate fabrics to prepare all appliqués for fusing.

4. Measure 8¾" from edge ('D' side) this will be the appliquéd tote flap. Refer to photo to position and fuse appliqués to flap area. Finish appliqué edges with machine satin stitch or other decorative stitching as desired.

5. Referring to step 2 diagram on page 89, sew unit from step 4 to lining piece, right sides together, along B, C, and D sides. Clip corners, turn and press.

6. Fuse stabilizer to batting piece following manufacturer's instructions. Trim piece slightly smaller than 16" x 36". Insert stabilizer/batting into unit from step 5. Hand stitch opening closed.

7. Quilt as desired. The stiffness of the stabilizer can make it difficult to maneuver the piece while quilting. Simple quilting is recommended.

8. Sew two 3½" x 42" Strap strips end-to-end to make one 3½"-wide continuous strip. Press. Make two. Trim strips to 64" or desired length and cut 3½"-wide batting strip to this same measurement.

9. Layer and center two 3½" x 64" strap strips right sides together on batting, wrong side of backing on batting. Using ¼"-wide seam, stitch around all edges, leaving a 4" opening on one side for turning as shown. Trim batting close to stitching and backing even with strap edge. Clip corners, turn, and press. Hand-stitch opening closed. Top stitch ¼" from edges and quilt as desired.

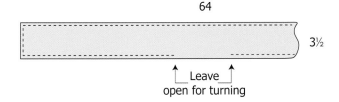

64

3½

Leave open for turning

10. With right sides together, measure and mark 12" from 'A' side as shown. Align strap end on this mark. Stitch using ¼"-wide seam starting ¼" from strap end. Repeat for other side, making sure strap is not twisted prior to sewing.

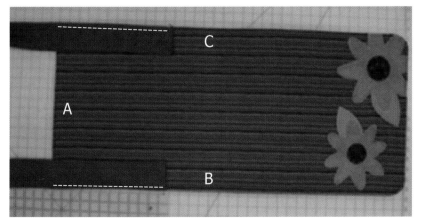

11. Pivot end of strap as shown in photo below. Sew across short strap end, starting and stopping stitching ¼" from strap side edges. Repeat for other side.

12. Rotate tote again to sew other side of strap to bag, reinforcing stitches. Repeat for other side.

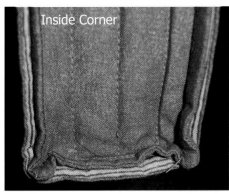

Inside Corner

13. Turn tote inside out. Photo shows finished strap and bag edge. Attach bag closure as desired.

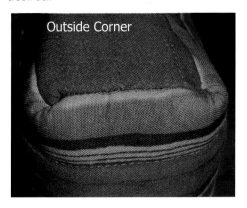

Outside Corner

Staying Centered
Laptop Tote
Large Flower
Make 1

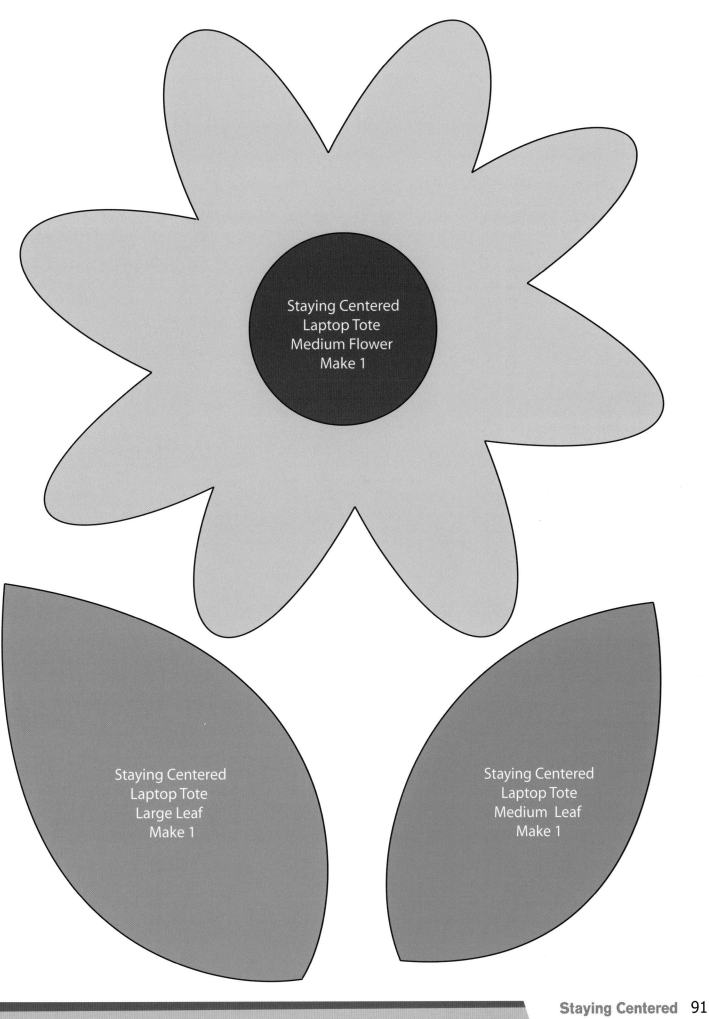

Staying Centered
Laptop Tote
Medium Flower
Make 1

Staying Centered
Laptop Tote
Large Leaf
Make 1

Staying Centered
Laptop Tote
Medium Leaf
Make 1

General
··· Directions

Cutting Strips and Pieces

We recommend washing cotton fabrics in cold water and pressing before making projects in this book. Using a rotary cutter, see-through ruler, and a cutting mat, cut the strips and pieces for the project. If indicated on the Cutting Chart, some will need to be cut again into smaller strips and pieces. Make second cuts in order shown to maximize use of fabric. The yardage amounts are based on an approximate fabric width of 42" and Fat Quarters are based on 18" x 22" pieces.

Pressing

Pressing is very important for accurate seam allowances. Press seams using either steam or dry heat with an "up and down" motion. Do not use side-to-side motion as this will distort the unit or block. Set the seam by pressing along the line of stitching, then press seams to one side as indicated by project instructions and diagram arrows.

Twisting Seams

When a block has several seams meeting in the center as shown, there will be less bulk if seam allowances are pressed in a circular type direction and the center intersection "twisted". Remove 1-2 stitches in the seam allowance to enable the center to twist and lay flat. This technique aids in quilt assembly by allowing the seams to fall opposite each other when repeated blocks are next to each other. The technique works well with 4-patch blocks, pinwheel blocks, and quarter-square triangle blocks.

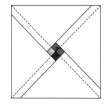

Accurate Seam Allowance

Accurate seam allowances are always important, but especially when the blocks contain many pieces and the quilt top contains multiple pieced borders. If each seam is off as little as ⅟₁₆", you'll soon find yourself struggling with components that just won't fit.

To ensure seams are a perfect ¼"-wide, try this simple test: Cut three strips of fabric, each exactly 1½" x 12". With right sides together, and long raw edges aligned, sew two strips together, carefully maintaining a ¼" seam. Press seam to one side. Add the third strip to complete the strip set. Press and measure. The finished strip set should measure 3½" x 12". The center strip should measure 1"-wide, the two outside strips 1¼"-wide, and the seam allowances exactly ¼".

If your measurements differ, check to make sure that seams have been pressed flat. If strip set still doesn't "measure up," try stitching a new strip set, adjusting the seam allowance until a perfect ¼"-wide seam is achieved.

Assembly Line Method

Whenever possible, use an assembly line method. Position pieces right sides together and line up next to sewing machine. Stitch first unit together, then continue sewing others without breaking threads. When all units are sewn, clip threads to separate. Press seams in direction of arrows as shown in step-by-step project diagrams.

Quick Corner Triangles

Quick corner triangles are formed by simply sewing fabric squares to other squares or rectangles. The directions and diagrams with each project illustrate what size pieces to use and where to place squares on the corresponding piece. Follow steps 1–3 below to make quick corner triangle units.

1. With pencil and ruler, draw diagonal line on wrong side of fabric square that will form the triangle. This will be your sewing line.

   Sewing line

2. With right sides together, place square on corresponding piece. Matching raw edges, pin in place, and sew ON drawn line. Trim off excess fabric, leaving ¼"-wide seam allowance as shown.

   Trim ¼" away from sewing line

3. Press seam in direction of arrow as shown in step-by-step project diagram. Measure completed quick corner triangle unit to ensure the greatest accuracy.

   Finished quick corner triangle unit

Fussy Cut

To make a "fussy cut," carefully position ruler or template over a selected design in fabric. Include seam allowances before cutting desired pieces.

Quick-Fuse Appliqué

Quick-fuse appliqué is a method of adhering appliqué pieces to a background with fusible web. For quick and easy results, simply quick-fuse appliqué pieces in place. Use sewable, lightweight fusible web for the projects in this book unless otherwise indicated. Finish raw edges with stitching as desired. Laundering is not recommended unless edges are finished.

1. With paper side up, lay fusible web over appliqué pattern. Leaving ½" space between pieces, trace all elements of design. Cut around traced pieces, approximately ¼" outside traced line.

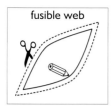

fusible web

2. With paper side up, position and press fusible web to wrong side of selected fabrics. Follow manufacturer's directions for iron temperature and fusing time. Cut out each piece on traced line.

fabric-wrong side

3. Remove paper backing from pieces. A thin film will remain on wrong side of fabric. Position and fuse all pieces of one appliqué design at a time onto background, referring to photos for placement. Fused design will be the reverse of traced pattern.

Appliqué Pressing Sheet

An appliqué pressing sheet is very helpful when there are many small elements to apply using a quick-fuse appliqué technique. The pressing sheet allows small items to be bonded together before applying them to the background. The sheet is coated with a special material that prevents fusible web from adhering permanently to the sheet. Follow manufacturer's directions. Remember to let fabric cool completely before lifting it from the appliqué sheet. If not cooled, the fusible web could remain on the sheet instead of on the fabric.

For accurate layout, place a line drawing of finished project under pressing sheet. Use this as a guide to adhere pieces.

Machine Appliqué

This technique should be used when you are planning to launder quick-fuse projects. Several different stitches can be used: small narrow zigzag stitch, satin stitch, blanket stitch, or another decorative machine stitch. Use an open toe appliqué foot if your machine has one. Use a stabilizer to obtain even stitches and help prevent puckering. Always practice first to check machine settings.

1. Fuse all pieces following Quick-Fuse Appliqué directions.

2. Cut a piece of stabilizer large enough to extend beyond the area to be stitched. Pin to the wrong side of fabric.

3. Select thread to match appliqué.

4. Following the order that appliqués were positioned, stitch along the edges of each section. Anchor beginning and ending stitches by tying off or stitching in place two or three times.

5. Complete all stitching, then remove stabilizer.

Hand Appliqué

Hand appliqué is easy when you start out with the right supplies. Cotton and machine embroidery thread are easy to work with. Pick a color that matches the appliqué fabric as closely as possible. Use appliqué or silk pins for holding shapes in place and a long, thin needle, such as a sharp, for stitching.

1. Make a template for every shape in the appliqué design. Use a dotted line to show where pieces overlap.

2. Place template on right side of appliqué fabric. Trace around template.

3. Cut out shapes ¼" beyond traced line.

4. Position shapes on background fabric, referring to quilt layout. Pin shapes in place.

5. When layering and stitching appliqué shapes, always work from background to foreground. Where shapes overlap, do not turn under and stitch edges of bottom pieces. Turn and stitch the edges of the piece on top.

6. Use the traced line as your turn-under guide. Entering from the wrong side of the appliqué shape, bring the needle up on the traced line. Using the tip of the needle, turn under the fabric along the traced line. Using blind stitch, stitch along folded edge to join the appliqué shape to the background fabric. Turn under and stitch about ¼" at a time.

Adding the Borders

1. Measure quilt through the center from side to side. Trim two border strips to this measurement. Sew to top and bottom of quilt. Press seams toward border.

2. Measure quilt through the center from top to bottom, including borders added in step 1. Trim border strips to this measurement. Sew to sides and press. Repeat to add additional borders.

Layering the Quilt

1. Cut backing and batting 4" to 8" larger than quilt top.

2. Lay pressed backing on bottom (right side down), batting in middle, and pressed quilt top (right side up) on top. Make sure everything is centered and that backing and batting are flat. Backing and batting will extend beyond quilt top.

3. Begin basting in center and work toward outside edges. Baste vertically and horizontally, forming a 3"–4" grid. Baste or pin completely around edge of quilt top. Quilt as desired. Remove basting.

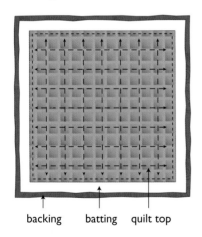

backing   batting   quilt top

Binding the Quilt

1. Trim batting and backing to ¼" beyond raw edge of quilt top. This will add fullness to binding.

2. Join binding strips to make one continuous strip if needed. To join, place 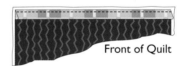 ←trim
strips perpendicular to each other, right sides together, and draw a diagonal line. Sew on drawn line and trim triangle extensions, leaving a ¼"-wide seam allowance. Continue stitching ends together to make the desired length. Press seams open.

3. Fold and press binding strips in half lengthwise with wrong sides together.

4. Measure quilt through center from side to side. Cut two binding strips to this measurement. Lay binding strips on top and bottom edges of quilt top with raw edges of binding and quilt top aligned. Sew through all layers, ¼" from quilt edge. Press binding away from quilt top.

Front of Quilt

5. Measure quilt through center from top to bottom, including binding just added. Cut two binding strips to this measurement and sew to sides through all layers, including binding just added. Press.

6. Folding top and bottom first, fold binding around to back then repeat with sides. Press and pin in position. Hand-stitch binding in place using a blind stitch.

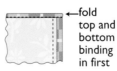 ←fold top and bottom binding in first

Mistyfuse™

When fusing several layers of fusible web to a project, the quilt can become very stiff and hard to quilt. We used a new product for this quilt called 'Mistyfuse'. It is a very lightweight adhesive that doesn't add stiffness or weight to the quilt when adhered. It can be used on all types of fabrics - velvets to cotton, and delicates like tulles and organza. Follow manufacturer's instructions when using this product. Some additional items you will need are freezer paper and parchment paper or an applique pressing sheet. For more information go to www.mistyfuse.com.

Finishing Pillows

1. Layer batting between pillow top and lining. Baste. Hand or machine quilt as desired. Trim batting and lining even with raw edge of pillow top.

2. Narrow hem one long edge of each backing piece by folding under ¼" to wrong side. Press. Fold under ¼" again to wrong side. Press. Stitch along folded edge.

3. With sides up, lay one backing piece over second piece so hemmed edges overlap, making backing unit the same measurement as the pillow top. Baste backing pieces together at top and bottom where they overlap.

4. With right sides together, position and pin pillow top to backing. Using ¼"-wide seam, sew around edges, trim corners, turn right side out, and press.

Tips for Felting Wool

1. Wet wool fabric or WoolFelt™ with hot water. Do not mix colors as dyes may run.

2. Blot wool with a dry towel and place both towel and wool in dryer on high heat until thoroughly dry. The result is a thicker, fuller fabric that will give added texture to the wool. Pressing felted wool is not recommended, as it will flatten the texture. Most wools will shrink 15-30% when felted, adjust yardage accordingly.

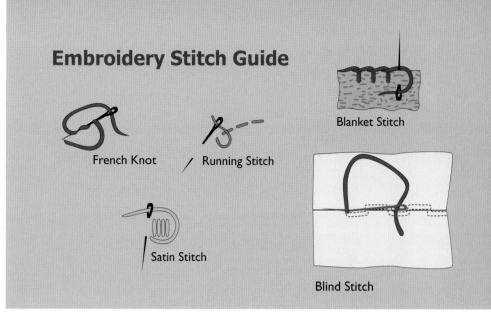

Embroidery Stitch Guide

French Knot

Running Stitch

Satin Stitch

Blanket Stitch

Blind Stitch

Circle Templates

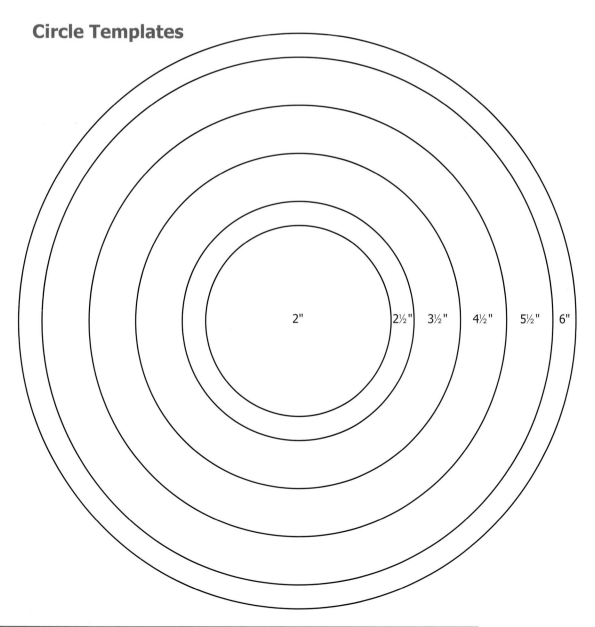

2" 2½" 3½" 4½" 5½" 6"

About Debbie Mumm

A talented designer, author, and entrepreneur, Debbie Mumm has been creating charming artwork and quilt designs for more than twenty years.

Debbie got her start in the quilting industry in 1986 with her unique and simple-to-construct quilt patterns. Since that time, she has authored more than fifty books featuring quilting and home decorating projects and has led her business to become a multi-faceted enterprise that includes publishing, fabric design, and licensed art divisions.

Known world-wide for the many licensed products that feature her designs, Debbie loves to bring traditional elements together with fresh palettes and modern themes to create the look of today's country.

Designs by Debbie Mumm

Special thanks to my creative teams:

Editorial & Project Design

Carolyn Ogden: Publications & Marketing Manager
Nancy Kirkland: Quilt Designer/Seamstress
Georgie Gerl: Technical Writer/Editor
Carolyn Lowe: Technical Editor • Kris Clifford: Paper Crafter
Anita Pederson: Machine Quilter

Book Design & Production

Monica Ziegler: Graphic Designer • Tom Harlow: Graphics Manager
Kris Clifford: Executive Assistant

Photography

Tom Harlow, Debbie Mumm® Graphics Studio
Carolyn Ogden: Photo Stylist

Art Team

Kathy Arbuckle: Artist/Designer • Gil-Jin Foster: Artist
Jackie Saling: Designer

The Debbie Mumm® Sewing Studio exclusively uses Bernina® sewing machines.

Discover More from Debbie Mumm®

*Debbie Mumm's®
HomeComings*

96-page, soft cover

*Debbie Mumm's®
Cuddle Quilts for
Little Girls and Boys*

96-page, soft cover

*Debbie Mumm's®
Colors from Nature*

96-page, soft cover

*Joy Joy Joy
by Debbie Mumm®*

96-page, soft cover

Produced by:
Debbie Mumm, Inc.
1116 E. Westview Court
Spokane, WA 99218
(509) 466-3572
Fax (509) 466-6919

www.debbiemumm.com

Published by:
Leisure Arts, Inc
5701 Ranch Drive
Little Rock, AR • 72223
www.leisurearts.com

Available at local fabric and craft shops or at
debbiemumm.com